THE THREE FORMS
OF UNITY

The Subordinate Doctrinal Standards of the
Reformed Church in the United States

The Creeds
The Heidelberg Catechism
The Belgic Confession of Faith
The Canons of Dort

The Reformed Church
in the United States
2011

COPYRIGHT

CONTENTS

Introduction

๛

THE UNITY of the Reformed Church in the U.S. (RCUS) consists to a large extent in its faithful adherence to a common faith and doctrine. The denomination affirms the great creeds of the early church—the Apostles', Nicene, and Athanasian Creeds—which define historic Christianity. It also subscribes to key doctrinal statements of the Protestant Reformation—the *Belgic Confession* (1561), the *Heidelberg Catechism* (1563), and the *Canons of Dort* (1618–19), which together are called the *Three Forms of Unity*.

The Bible exhorts us to promote the unity of the church through common beliefs: "There is one body and one Spirit, just as you were called in one hope of your calling; one Lord, one faith, one baptism; one God and Father of all, who is above all, and through all, and in you all" (Eph. 4:1–6). It also calls us to have a unity of heart and mind; "Therefore if there is any consolation in Christ, if any comfort of love, if any fellowship of the Spirit, if any affection and mercy, fulfill my joy by being like-minded, having the same love, being of one accord, of one mind" (Phil. 2:1–3).

Faith is a personal act that has as its content a body of objective truths which we confess in unity with other Christians. The New Testament speaks of "the faith which was once for all delivered to the saints" (Jude 3; cf. Acts 6:7, 14:22; Gal. 1:23). Biblical faith is intelligible and can be theologically articulated in creed, catechism, and confession.

Creeds of the Early Church

The word "creed" (Latin, *credo*) means "I believe," and reflects the biblical emphasis on salvation by faith. The early creeds grew out of the rudimentary forms of confession we find in the New Testament, for example, in 1 Tim 3:14–16:

> God was manifested in the flesh,
> Justified in the Spirit,
> Seen by angels,
> Preached among the Gentiles,
> Believed on in the world,
> Received up in glory.

Paul exhorted the young pastor Timothy to "hold fast the pattern of sound words which you have heard from me, in faith and love which are in Christ Jesus. That good thing which was committed to you, keep by the Holy Spirit who dwells in us" (2 Tim. 1:13–14). Pastors especially are to embrace, guard, and protect the apostolic standard of doctrine as a valuable treasure committed to their care.

The early church understood these matters and began to articulate the content of its beliefs in contrast to the multiple heresies it faced. Building on the Trinitarian baptismal formula in Matt. 28:19, it stated the essential doctrines of the faith.

A creed came to be understood as a concise, ecclesiastically authorized statement of the fundamental points of Christian doctrine. The Apostles', Nicene, and Athanasian Creeds have often been called "ecumenical," meaning general or universal, because they have been accepted by all true, historic Christian churches.

THE HEIDELBERG CATECHISM

"Catechism" is a biblical term (*katacheo*). Used at least seven times in the New Testament, it refers to instruction in the faith. Although the question-and-answer form of a catechism is not found in the Bible, the general injunction to train converts and covenant children is given to the church (Matt. 28:19–20).

The Church throughout the ages has taken this responsibility seriously. In preparing converts or children to make a public profession of faith, the Heidelberg Catechism has provided written questions on the Apostle's Creed, the Ten Commandments, and the Lord's Prayer. Frederick the III stated this as his reason for commissioning the writing of the Heidelberg Catechism:

> And accordingly … we have secured the preparation of a summary course of instruction or catechism of our Christian Religion, according to the word of God … in order that the youth in churches and schools may be piously instructed in such Christian doctrine, and be thoroughly trained therein, but also that the Pastors and Schoolmasters themselves may be provided with a fixed form and model, by which to regulate the instruction of youth, and not, at their option, adopt daily changes, or introduce erroneous doctrine. (Preface to the *Heidelberg Catechism*, 1563)

Our commitment to the Heidelberg Catechism enables us to provide clear training for the youth of the Church, giving a balanced and succinct treatment of what a Christian is to believe and how he is to live.

CONFESSIONS OF THE REFORMATION

A confession is similar to a creed. It is also biblical term (*homologia*), and means that we "say the same thing" or affirm a statement that has previously been made. The pattern of confession is provided by Christ

Himself, who witnessed a good confession before Pilate that He was the Christ and the King (1 Tim. 6:13, Mk. 15:13, Jn. 18:36–37). The first great confession in the New Testament was made by Peter in answer to Christ's question, "Who do men say that I, the Son of Man, am?" Peter's affirmation focused on the Person of Jesus Christ: He is the Messiah and the Son of the living God (cf. 1 Jn. 4:15, 2 Jn. 7).

It is our duty not only to believe as a personal act before God, but to verbally confess this before men (Matt. 10:32, Lk. 12:8, Rom. 10:9). A confession of faith means to declare publicly before many witnesses that an individual or a congregation pledges allegiance to Jesus Christ as Lord. Always more than mental assent, it is a covenant commitment to follow Him. In it, a person is willing to state what he believes, even if it means suffering persecution (Matt. 10:32–39, Jn. 9:22, 12:42).

The Reformed Church in the U.S. embraces two confessional documents from the period of the Reformation. The first, the *Belgic Confession*, covers in some detail the whole range of biblical doctrine. Written in a lively style, it captures the main points of Reformed theology.

The second, the *Canons of Dort*, focuses on the true way to understand the gospel of salvation by grace alone, through faith alone, in Christ alone, and for the glory of God alone. It helps us understand that there is nothing in us, or that can be done by us, to save ourselves. We are wholly dependent on God's sovereign grace to impart faith and preserve us in it.

NECESSITY OF CREEDS AND CONFESSIONS

Some question whether a creed, confession, or catechism is necessary. Is it not sufficient, they say, to just believe the Bible and have "no creed but Christ"? Although this seems laudable, Christ exhorts us, "Therefore whoever confesses Me before men, him I will also confess before My Father who is in heaven" (Matt. 10:32–33, Lk. 12:8–9). Paul elaborates further when he connects faith and confession: "that if you confess with your mouth the Lord Jesus and believe in your heart that God has raised Him from the dead, you will be saved" (Rom. 10:9–10). The Scriptures give us both the warrant and even the duty to confess our faith publicly before men.

Some say that they have no creed or confession. But whenever they state what they understand the Bible to teach, they are in fact making a confession. Many immature Christians are deceived by such rhetoric and are "tossed to and fro and carried about with every wind of doctrine, by the trickery of men, in the cunning craftiness of deceitful plotting" (Eph. 4:14).

As our culture embraces post-modern views we see the wholesale rejection of truth itself. There are those who hide under the cover of ambiguity, while either continually modifying their opinions, or secretly embracing heretical opinions. Their real objection to confessions is an unwillingness to submit to any ecclesiastical authority. They will not commit themselves to a theological tradition which maintains historic biblical orthodoxy.

The RCUS is glad to publish what it believes. It views its confessional documents not as outmoded forms of archaic theology nor interesting museum pieces. It does not see the need for continual revision of its confessions or the need to add a "contemporary testimony" in the form of a prose-poem. In the historic, orthodox creeds and Reformed confessions it finds continuity with the true church of the past and a true unity among its churches today.

ULTIMATE AND SUBORDINATE STANDARDS

The RCUS does not, however, make its confessional statements equal to, or elevated above, Scripture. Our *Constitution* says,

> The Holy Scriptures of the Old and New Testaments, which are called canonical, being recognized as genuine and inspired, are received as the true and proper Word of God, infallible and inerrant, and the ultimate rule and measure of the whole Christian faith and doctrine. (*Constitution*, Art. 176)

Mere human writings can never be our ultimate and final standard, even those with higher authority due to the fact that they were decided in the councils of the church. The Belgic Confession itself states this:

> Neither may we consider any writings of men, however holy these men may have been, of equal value with those divine Scriptures, nor ought we to consider custom, or the great multitude, or antiquity, or succession of times and persons, or councils, decrees or statutes, as of equal value with the truth of God, since the truth is above all. (*Belgic Confession*, Art. 7)

This is an integral part of our confession—to define the nature of biblical authority and to distinguish it from confessional statements. Our creeds, confessions, and catechism are to be understood as *subordinate* standards. And yet they have real authority in the church because they are based upon and embody biblical truth.

> The Heidelberg Catechism, the Belgic Confession of Faith, and the Canons of Dort are received as authoritative expressions of the truths taught in the Holy Scriptures, and are acknowledged to be the subordinate standards of doctrine in the Reformed Church in the United States. (*Constitution*, Art. 177)

INTERPRETATION OF THE BIBLE

The *Three Forms of Unity* explain the way in which we interpret the Scriptures (*Constitution*, Art. 177). Biblical interpretation is the right of the Church, meeting at properly called councils (Acts 16:6 ff). A merely private effort to create one's own confession does not have the seal of the Church upon it. Authoritative doctrinal formulations are made in the context of the church's struggle with heresy, when it clarifies critical theological issues and affirms what the Bible truly teaches.

Because of this, the RCUS does not start anew, as if it were the first to seriously study the Bible or articulate its faith. It therefore takes its stand with historic Christian orthodoxy and the Reformed confessions in the one, true faith. We unite ourselves to the true Church in ages past, to that line of biblical orthodoxy which we believe is most faithful to Scripture. We affirm that "Jesus Christ is the same yesterday, today, and forever" (Heb. 13:8).

CONFESSIONAL SUBSCRIPTION AND TEACHING

Our Constitution, which incorporates the *Reformed Standards of Unity*, provides guidance for what should be taught in the church. Our doctrinal standards are a living confession in the life of the church. Each RCUS congregation is bound to confess these as the expression of its being of the same mind with the rest of the church (*Constitution*, Art. 7).

When men are licensed to the gospel ministry or installed as teachers of theology, they are to subscribe to the *Three Forms* by signing their name to the following:

> "I hereby testify that I honestly and truly accept the doctrine of the Heidelberg Catechism, the Belgic Confession of Faith, and the Canons of Dort as in accordance with the teaching of the Holy Scriptures, and promise faithfully to preach and defend the same." (*Constitution*, Art. 22)

In fact, to manifest the unity of the faith we also believe that members should be taught to confess our *Three Forms* as the faithful interpretation of Scripture (*Constitution*, Art. 4). It is especially incumbent upon the pastors and elders of the congregations to see that the youth of the church are properly instructed in the basic teachings of the Christian faith (*Constitution*, Art. 182). Therefore,

> Every pastor shall carefully prepare the youth in his pastoral charge for communicant membership in the Church by diligently instructing them in the doctrines and duties of the Christian religion. The period of instruction shall, if possible, be so extended that the pupils memorize and are able to recite the entire Heidelberg Catechism before confirmation. The course of

instruction shall include catechetical explanation and memorization, Bible history, Bible readings and memorizations, and the study of the books and contents of the Bible, the Belgic Confession of Faith, the Canons of Dort, church history, also the singing and memorization of Psalms, hymns, and Scripture songs. (*Constitution*, Art. 192)

We, therefore, commend to you these doctrinal standards of the Reformed Church in the U.S. for your careful, prayerful study and believe that you will find them to be a full and faithful summary of what Scripture teaches.

"… till we all come to the unity of the faith and of the knowledge of the Son of God, to a perfect man, to the measure of the stature of the fullness of Christ" (Eph. 4:13).

Note on the Text

In this edition of the *Three Forms of Unity*, some additions and revisions have been made, which are more a matter of form than of substance. The revision was undertaken under the direction of the 264th Synod of the Reformed Church in the U.S. (2010) through its Publications and Promotions Committee.

In agreement with the Belgic Confession (Art. 9), we have included three important creeds from the early Church: the Apostles' Creed, the Nicene Creed, and the Athanasian Creed. The text of the Belgic Confession and the Canons of Dort was originally taken from the *Psalter Hymnal, Doctrinal Standards and Liturgy of the Christian Reformed Church* (Grand Rapids, 1959). Certain modifications were made by various Synods of the RCUS to reflect its commitment to biblical consistency.

The CRC text used both the Revised Standard (RSV) and Authorized (KJV) versions of the Bible for scripture references. In this edition, all Bible quotations and allusions have been conformed to *The New King James Version* (Thomas Nelson, Inc., 1982). The Bible is referenced in three ways: (a) direct quotations, (b) allusions, and (c) quote fragments. All direct quotations in the Belgic Confession and Canons of Dort are set in italics, whereas Scriptural allusions are set in regular type, followed by the reference note. These have been incorporated in light of proper English grammar and syntax.

THE CREEDS

THE APOSTLES' CREED

"What, then, is necessary for a Christian to believe?" asks the Heidelberg Catechism. "All that is promised us in the gospel, which the articles of our catholic, undoubted Christian faith teach us in summary," is the reply. Though this creed was not penned by the Apostles, it summarizes the Bible's teaching with simplicity, brevity, and beauty. Originally used as a baptismal formula in the second century, it reached its present form in the sixth. It gives a concise expression of the fundamentals of historic Christianity.

I believe in GOD THE FATHER Almighty,
Maker of heaven and earth.

And in JESUS CHRIST,
His only-begotten Son, our Lord:
who was conceived by the Holy Spirit,
born of the virgin Mary,
suffered under Pontius Pilate,
was crucified, dead, and buried;
He descended into hell;
the third day He rose from the dead;
He ascended into heaven,
and sits at the right hand of
God the Father Almighty;
from there He shall come to judge
the living and the dead.

I believe in the HOLY SPIRIT,
the holy, catholic Church,
the communion of saints,
the forgiveness of sins,
the resurrection of the body,
and the life everlasting.

AMEN.

THE NICENE CREED

This creed is an accurate and majestic formulation of the historic faith of orthodox Christianity. Originating at the Council of Nicea (AD 325) and revised at the Council of Constantinople (AD 381), it affirmed the biblical doctrine of the Trinity and the Person of Christ in opposition to various heresies, especially Arianism. The Western Church added the article on the procession of the Holy Spirit from Christ, "and the Son" (Latin: *filioque*) when it was adopted in its present form at the Council of Toledo (AD 589).

ɞ

I believe in one GOD, THE FATHER Almighty, Maker of heaven and earth, and of all things visible and invisible.

And in one LORD JESUS CHRIST, the only-begotten Son of God, begotten of the Father before all worlds; God of God, Light of Light, very God of very God; begotten, not made, being of one substance with the Father, by whom all things were made.

Who, for us men and for our salvation, came down from heaven, and was incarnate by the Holy Spirit of the virgin Mary, and was made man; and was crucified also for us under Pontius Pilate; He suffered and was buried; and the third day He rose again, according to the Scriptures; and ascended into heaven, and sits on the right hand of the Father; and He shall come again, with glory, to judge the living and the dead; whose kingdom shall have no end.

And I believe in the HOLY SPIRIT, the Lord and Giver of life; who proceeds from the Father and the Son; who with the Father and the Son together is worshiped and glorified; who spoke by the prophets.

And I believe one holy catholic and apostolic Church. I acknowledge one baptism for the remission of sins; and I look for the resurrection of the dead, and the life of the world to come.

AMEN.

THE ATHANASIAN CREED

This creed has been named after Athanasius (AD 293–373), the champion of orthodoxy against the Arian heresy. Although he did not write it, the name persists because it was commonly ascribed to him by the Medieval Church. Being of Western origin, the creed first appeared in the early sixth century. Although the author is unknown, it embodies the teaching of Augustine (AD 354–430) in his book *De Trinitate*, as well as the decisions of the Council of Chalcedon on the Person of Christ (AD 451). Written in rhythmic cadences, this creed has been chanted in public worship by some churches. It is the fullest ecclesiastical statement of the truths of the Trinity and the Person of Christ.

&

THE TRINITY

[1] Whosoever will be saved, before all things it is necessary that he hold the catholic faith; [2] Which faith unless every one do keep whole and undefiled, without doubt he shall perish everlastingly.

[3] And the catholic faith is this: That we worship one God in Trinity, and Trinity in Unity; [4] Neither confounding the persons, nor dividing the substance. [5] For there is one person of the Father, another of the Son, and another of the Holy Spirit. [6] But the Godhead of the Father, of the Son, and of the Holy Spirit is all one, the glory equal, the majesty co-eternal.

[7] Such as the Father is, such is the Son, and such is the Holy Spirit. [8] The Father uncreated, the Son uncreated, and the Holy Spirit uncreated. [9] The Father incomprehensible, the Son incomprehensible, and the Holy Spirit incomprehensible. [10] The Father eternal, the Son eternal, and the Holy Spirit eternal. [11] And yet they are not three eternals, but one eternal. [12] As also there are not three uncreated nor three incomprehensibles, but one uncreated and one incomprehensible. [13] So likewise the Father is almighty, the Son almighty, and the Holy Spirit almighty; [14] And yet they are not three almighties, but one almighty.

[15] So the Father is God, the Son is God, and the Holy Spirit is God; [16] And yet they are not three Gods, but one God. [17] So likewise the Father is Lord, the Son Lord, and the Holy Spirit Lord; [18] And yet they are not three Lords, but one Lord. [19] For like as we are compelled by the Christian truth to acknowledge every Person by himself to be God and Lord; [20] So are we forbidden by the catholic religion to say: There are three Gods or three Lords.

[21] The Father is made of none, neither created nor begotten. [22] The Son is of the Father alone; not made nor created, but begotten. [23] The Holy Spirit is of the Father and of the Son; neither made, nor created, nor begotten, but proceeding. [24] So there is one Father, not three Fathers; one Son, not three Sons; one Holy Spirit, not three Holy Spirits. [25] And in this Trinity none is before, or after another; none is greater, or less than another. [26] But the whole three persons are co-eternal, and co-equal. [27] So that in all things, as said before, the Unity in Trinity and the Trinity in Unity is to be worshipped. [28] He therefore that will be saved must thus think of the Trinity.

THE PERSON OF CHRIST

[29] Furthermore it is necessary to everlasting salvation that he also believe rightly the incarnation of our Lord Jesus Christ. [30] For the right faith is that we believe and confess that our Lord Jesus Christ, the Son of God, is God and man. [31] God of the substance of the Father, begotten before the worlds; and man of the substance of His mother, born in the world. [32] Perfect God and perfect man, of a reasonable soul and human flesh subsisting. [33] Equal to the Father as touching His Godhead, and inferior to the Father as touching His manhood.

[34] Who, although He is God and man, yet He is not two, but one Christ. [35] One, not by conversion of the Godhead into flesh, but by taking of the manhood into God. [36] One altogether, not by confusion of substance, but by unity of person. [37] For as the reasonable soul and flesh is one man, so God and man is one Christ; [38] Who suffered for our salvation, descended into hell, rose again the third day from the dead; [39] He ascended into heaven, He sits on the right hand of the Father, God Almighty; [40] From there He shall come to judge the living and the dead. [41] At whose coming all men shall rise again with their bodies; [42] And shall give account of their own works. [43] And they that have done good shall go into life everlasting, and they that have done evil into everlasting fire.

[44] This is the catholic faith, which unless a man believe faithfully, he cannot be saved.

AMEN.

ରେ

THE HEIDELBERG CATECHISM

MODERN ENGLISH VERSION

ଔ

Introduction

ଦ୍ଧ

THIS CATECHISM, or instruction in the Christian faith, received its name from the place of its origin, Heidelberg, Germany, the capital of the Electorate of the Palatinate. That the Reformed faith might be taught and maintained in his domain, the godly elector Frederick III commissioned Zacharias Ursinus, professor at the Heidelberg University, and Caspar Olevianus, court preacher, to prepare a manual for instructing the youth and guiding pastors and teachers in the basic doctrines of the Christian faith. Prepared with the advice and cooperation of the entire theological faculty, heartily approved by the Elector himself, and sanctioned by the Synodical gathering of prominent Reformed preachers and theologians, it was first published in Heidelberg with a preface dated January 19, 1563.

The Great Synod of Dort (1618–1619) declared that the Heidelberg Catechism was in all respects in harmony with the Word of God and it required office-bearers to subscribe to it. It was called "an admirably composed compendium of the orthodox Christian doctrine, wisely adapted to the comprehension of tender youths, and also to the more elaborate instruction of adults." The Synod issued directives for it to be used by parents in teaching their children, by instructors in the schools, and by pastors on each Lord's Day afternoon.

It has been, deservedly, the most widely used and influential catechism of the Reformation period. The Reformed Churches of Germany, the Netherlands, Hungary, Transylvania, and Poland adopted it. Among the thirty languages into which the catechism has been translated are Dutch, English, French, Polish, Hungarian, Greek, Lithuanian, Hebrew, Italian, Bohemian, Javanese, Arabic, Singalese, and Malay. In North America it was adopted as a standard of the Reformed Church in the United States from the very beginning of its history.

In 1820 the first English version of the Catechism appeared in the United States. In 1863 a new English translation was made, called the Tercentenary Version. The Reformed Church in the U.S. further revised this edition in 1950. Additional Bible references (marked with an asterisk *) were then added. Subsequently, a modern English revision was made which has been identified as "Edition 1979" on the title page. First made by a special committee of the Eureka Classis, it was not printed until directed by the 1986 Synod. In 2011 the Scripture references and allusions were updated to the *New King James Version* of the Bible along with some minor textual changes and corrections.

It is our sincere prayer that this edition may turn the attention of readers and students with renewed interest to the immeasurable blessings of that "only comfort in life and in death."

THE HEIDELBERG CATECHISM

MODERN ENGLISH VERSION

ဢ

Introduction

LORD'S DAY 1

1. What is your only comfort in life and in death?

That I, with body and soul, both in life and in death,[1] am not my own,[2] but belong to my faithful Savior Jesus Christ,[3] who with His precious blood[4] has fully satisfied for all my sins,[5] and redeemed me from all the power of the devil;[6] and so preserves me[7] that without the will of my Father in heaven not a hair can fall from my head;[8] indeed, that all things must work together for my salvation.[9] Wherefore, by His Holy Spirit, He also assures me of eternal life,[10] and makes me heartily willing and ready from now on to live unto Him.[11]

[1] Rom. 14:7–8. [2] 1 Cor. 6:19. [3] 1 Cor. 3:23. [4] 1 Pet. 1:18–19. [5] 1 Jn. 1:7; 2:2. [6] 1 Jn. 3:8. [7] Jn. 6:39. [8] Matt. 10:29–30; Lk. 21:18. [9] Rom. 8:28. [10] 2 Cor. 1:21–22; Eph. 1:13–14; Rom. 8:16. [11] Rom. 8:1.

2. How many things are necessary for you to know, that in this comfort you may live and die happily?

Three things:[1] First, the greatness of my sin and misery.[2] Second, how I am redeemed from all my sins and misery.[3] Third, how I am to be thankful to God for such redemption.[4]

[1] Lk. 24:46–47; 1 Cor. 6:11; Tit. 3:3–7. [2] Jn. 9:41; 15:22. [3] Jn. 17:3. [4] Eph. 5:8–11; 1 Pet. 2:9–12; Rom. 6:11–14; *Rom. 7:24–25; *Gal. 3:13; *Col. 3:17.

FIRST PART: MAN'S MISERY

LORD'S DAY 2

3. From where do you know your misery?

From the Law of God.[1]

[1] Rom. 3:20; *Rom. 7:7.

4. **What does the Law of God require of us?**

    Christ teaches us in sum, Matthew 22, "You shall love the Lord
    your God with all your heart, with all your soul, and with all your
    mind. This is the first and great commandment. And the second
    is like it: You shall love your neighbor as yourself. On these two
    commandments hang all the Law and the Prophets."[1]

    [1] Matt. 22:37–40; Lk. 10:27. *Deut. 6:5. *Gal. 5:14.

5. **Can you keep all this perfectly?**

    No,[1] for I am prone by nature to hate God and my neighbor.[2]

    [1] Rom. 3:10–12, 23; 1 Jn. 1:8, 10. [2] Rom. 8:7; Eph. 2:3.

LORD'S DAY 3

6. **Did God create man thus, wicked and perverse?**

    No,[1] but God created man good and after His own image,[2] that
    is, in righteousness and true holiness, that he might rightly know
    God his Creator, heartily love Him, and live with Him in eternal
    blessedness, to praise and glorify Him.[3]

    [1] Gen. 1:31. [2] Gen. 1:26–27. [3] 2 Cor. 3:18; Col. 3:10; Eph. 4:24.

7. **From where, then, does this depraved nature of man come?**

    From the fall and disobedience of our first parents, Adam and Eve,
    in Paradise,[1] whereby our nature became so corrupt that we are all
    conceived and born in sin.[2]

    [1] Gen. 3 (The whole chapter). Rom. 5:12, 18–19. [2] Ps. 51:5; *Ps. 14:2–3.

8. **But are we so depraved that we are completely incapable of any
    good and prone to all evil?**

    Yes,[1] unless we are born again by the Spirit of God.[2]

    [1] Jn. 3:6; Gen. 6:5; Job 14:4; Isa. 53:6. [2] Jn. 3:5; *Gen. 8:21; *2 Cor. 3:5; *Rom. 7:18;
    *Jer. 17:9.

LORD'S DAY 4

9. **Does not God, then, do injustice to man by requiring of him in
    His Law that which he cannot perform?**

    No, for God so made man that he could perform it;[1] but man,
    through the instigation of the devil, by willful disobedience
    deprived himself and all his descendants of those divine gifts.[2]

    [1] Eph. 4:24. [2] Rom. 5:12.

10. Will God allow such disobedience and apostasy to go unpunished?

Certainly not,[1] but He is terribly displeased with our inborn as well as our actual sins, and will punish them in just judgment in time and eternity, as He has declared, "Cursed is everyone who does not continue in all things which are written in the book of the law, to do them."

[1] Heb. 9:27. [2] Deut. 27:26; Gal. 3:10; *Rom. 1:18; *Matt. 25:41.

11. But is not God also merciful?

God is indeed merciful,[1] but He is likewise just;[2] His justice therefore requires that sin which is committed against the most high majesty of God, be punished with extreme, that is, with everlasting punishment both of body and soul.

[1] Ex. 34:6–7. [2] Ex. 20:5; Ps. 5:5–6; 2 Cor. 6:14–16; *Rev. 14:11.

Second Part: Man's Redemption

Lord's Day 5

12. Since, then, by the righteous judgment of God we deserve temporal and eternal punishment, how may we escape this punishment and be again received into favor?

God wills that His justice be satisfied;[1] therefore, we must make full satisfaction to that justice, either by ourselves or by another.[2]

[1] Ex. 20:5; 23:7. [2] Rom. 8:3–4.

13. Can we ourselves make this satisfaction?

Certainly not; on the contrary, we daily increase our guilt.[1]

[1] Job 9:2–3; 15:15–16; Matt. 6:12; *16:26.

14. Can any mere creature make satisfaction for us?

None; for first, God will not punish any other creature for the sin which man committed;[1] and further, no mere creature can sustain the burden of God's eternal wrath against sin[2] and redeem others from it.

[1] Heb. 2:14–18. [2] Ps. 130:3.

15. What kind of mediator and redeemer, then, must we seek?

One who is a true[1] and righteous man,[2] and yet more powerful than all creatures, that is, one who is also true God.[3]

[1] 1 Cor. 15:21–22, 25–26. [2] Jer. 13:16; Isa. 53:11; 2 Cor. 5:21; Heb. 7:15–16.
[3] Isa. 7:14; Heb. 7:26.

LORD'S DAY 6

16.   Why must He be a true and righteous man?

Because the justice of God requires[1] that the same human nature
which has sinned should make satisfaction for sin; but one who is
himself a sinner cannot satisfy for others.[2]

[1] Rom: 5:15. [2] Isa. 53:3–5.

17.   Why must He also be true God?

That by the power of His Godhead He might bear in His manhood
the burden of God's wrath,[1] and so obtain for[2] and restore to us
righteousness and life.[3]

[1] Isa. 53:8; Acts 2:24. [2] Jn. 3:16; Acts 20:28. [3] 1 Jn. 1:2.

18.   But who now is that Mediator, who in one person is true God and also a true and righteous man?

Our Lord Jesus Christ,[1] who is freely given unto us for complete
redemption and righteousness.[2]

[1] Matt. 1:23; 1 Tim. 3:16; Lk. 2:11. [2] 1 Cor. 1:30; *Acts 4:12.

19.   From where do you know this?

From the Holy Gospel, which God Himself first revealed in
Paradise,[1] afterwards proclaimed by the holy patriarchs[2] and
prophets, and foreshadowed by the sacrifices and other ceremonies
of the law,[3] and finally fulfilled by His well-beloved Son.[4]

[1] Gen. 3:15. [2] Gen. 22:18; 49:10–11; Rom. 1:2; Heb. 1:1; Acts 3:22–24; 10:43. [3] Jn.
5:46. Heb. 10:7. [4] Rom. 10:4; Gal. 4:4–5; *Heb. 10:1.

LORD'S DAY 7

20.   Are all men, then, saved by Christ as they have perished in Adam?

No, only those who by true faith are engrafted into Him and receive
all His benefits.[1]

[1] Jn. 1:12–13; 1 Cor. 15:22; Ps. 2:12; Rom. 11:20; Heb. 4:2–3; 10:39.

21.   What is true faith?

True faith is not only a sure knowledge whereby I hold for truth all that God has revealed to us in His Word,[1] but also a hearty trust,[2] which the Holy Spirit[3] works in me by the Gospel,[4] that not only to others, but to me also, forgiveness of sins, everlasting righteousness, and salvation are freely given by God,[5] merely of grace, only for the sake of Christ's merits.[6]

[1] Jas. 1:6. [2] Rom. 4:16–18; 5:1. [3] 2 Cor. 4:13; Phil. 1:19, 29. [4] Rom. 1:16; 10:17. [5] Heb. 11:1–2; Rom. 1:17. [6] Eph. 2:7–9; Rom. 3:24–25; Gal. 2:16; *Acts 10:43.

22. What, then, is necessary for a Christian to believe?

All that is promised us in the Gospel,[1] which the articles of our catholic, undoubted Christian faith teach us in summary.

[1] Jn. 20:31; Matt. 28:20. *2 Pet. 1:21; *2 Tim. 3:15.

23. What are these articles?

I believe in GOD THE FATHER Almighty, Maker of heaven and earth.

And in JESUS CHRIST, His only-begotten Son, our Lord: who was conceived by the Holy Spirit, born of the virgin Mary, suffered under Pontius Pilate, was crucified, dead, and buried; He descended into hell; the third day He rose from the dead; He ascended into heaven, and sits at the right hand of God the Father Almighty; From there He will come to judge the living and the dead.

I believe in the HOLY SPIRIT, the holy, catholic Church, the communion of saints, the forgiveness of sins, the resurrection of the body, and the life everlasting.

LORD'S DAY 8

24. How are these articles divided?

Into three parts: the first is of God the Father and our creation; the second, of God the Son and our redemption; the third, of God the Holy Spirit and our sanctification.[1]

[1] 1 Pet. 1:2; *1 Jn. 5:7.

25. Since there is but one Divine Being,[1] why do you speak of three persons: Father, Son, and Holy Spirit?

Because God has so revealed Himself in His Word,[2] that these three distinct persons are the one, true, eternal God.

[1] Deut. 6:4. [2] Isa. 61:1; Ps. 110:1; Matt. 3:16–17; 28:19; 1 Jn. 5:7; *2 Cor. 13:14.

God the Father

Lord's Day 9

26. What do you believe when you say, "I believe in God the Father Almighty, Maker of heaven and earth"?

That the eternal Father of our Lord Jesus Christ, who of nothing made heaven and earth with all that is in them,[1] who likewise upholds, and governs them by His eternal counsel and providence,[2] is for the sake of Christ, His Son, my God and my Father,[3] in whom I so trust as to have no doubt that He will provide me with all things necessary for body and soul;[4] and further, that whatever evil He sends upon me in this valley of tears, He will turn to my good;[5] for He is able to do it, being Almighty God,[6] and willing also, being a faithful Father.[7]

[1] Gen. 1:31; Ps. 33:6; *Col. 1:16; *Heb. 11:3. [2] Ps. 104:2–5; Matt. 10:30; Heb. 1:3; Ps. 115:3; *Acts 17:24–25. [3] Jn. 1:12; Rom. 8:15; Gal. 4:5–7; Eph. 1:5; *Eph. 3:14–16; *Matt. 6:8. [4] Ps. 55:22; Matt. 6:25–26; Lk. 12:22–24; Ps. 90:1–2. [5] Rom. 8:28; *Acts 17:27–28. [6] Rom. 10:12. [7] Matt. 7:9–11; *Num. 23:19.

Lord's Day 10

27. What do you understand by the providence of God?

The almighty, everywhere-present power of God,[1] whereby, as it were by His hand, He still upholds heaven and earth with all creatures,[2] and so governs them that herbs and grass, rain and drought, fruitful and barren years, meat and drink,[3] health and sickness,[4] riches and poverty,[5] indeed, all things come not by chance, but by His fatherly hand.

[1] Acts 17:25–26. [2] Heb. 1:3. [3] Jer. 5:24; *Acts 14:17. [4] Jn. 9:3. [5] Prov. 22:2; *Ps. 103:19; Rom. 5:3–5a.

28. What does it profit us to know that God created, and by His providence upholds, all things?

That we may be patient in adversity,[1] thankful in prosperity,[2] and for what is future have good confidence in our faithful God and Father, that no creature shall separate us from His love,[3] since all creatures are so in His hand, that without His will they cannot so much as move.[4]

[1] Rom. 5:3; Jas. 1:3; Job 1:21. [2] Deut. 8:10; 1 Thess. 5:18. [3] Rom. 8:35, 38–39. [4] Job 1:12; Acts 17:25–28; Prov. 21:1; *Ps. 71:7; *2 Cor. 1:10.

God the Son

LORD'S DAY 11

29. Why is the Son of God called "Jesus," that is, Savior?

Because He saves us from all our sins,[1] and because salvation is not to be sought or found in any other.[2]

[1] Matt. 1:21; Heb. 7:25. [2] Acts 4:12; *Lk. 2:10–11.

30. Do those also believe in the only Savior Jesus, who seek their salvation and welfare from "saints," themselves, or anywhere else?

No; although they make their boast of Him, yet in their deeds they deny the only Savior Jesus;[1] for either Jesus is not a complete Savior, or they who by true faith receive this Savior, must have in Him all that is necessary to their salvation.[2]

[1] 1 Cor. 1:13, 30–31; Gal. 5:4. [2] Isa. 9:7; Col. 1:20; 2:10; Jn. 1:16; *Matt. 23:28.

LORD'S DAY 12

31. Why is He called "Christ," that is, Anointed?

Because He is ordained of God the Father and anointed with the Holy Spirit[1] to be our chief Prophet and Teacher,[2] who has fully revealed to us the secret counsel and will of God concerning our redemption;[3] and our only High Priest,[4] who by the one sacrifice of His body, has redeemed us, and ever lives to make intercession for us with the Father;[5] and our eternal King, who governs us by His Word and Spirit, and defends and preserves us in the redemption obtained for us.[6]

[1] Heb. 1:9. [2] Deut. 18:15; Acts 3:22. [3] Jn. 1:18; 15:15. [4] Ps. 110:4; Heb. 7:21. [5] Rom. 5:9–10. [6] Ps. 2:6; Lk. 1:33; Matt. 28:18; *Isa. 61:1–2; *1 Pet. 2:24; *Rev. 19:16.

32. But why are you called a Christian?

Because by faith I am a member of Christ[1] and thus a partaker of His anointing,[2] in order that I also may confess His Name,[3] may present myself a living sacrifice of thankfulness to Him,[4] and with a free conscience may fight against sin and the devil in this life,[5] and hereafter in eternity reign with Him over all creatures.[6]

[1] Acts 11:26; 1 Jn. 2:27; *1 Jn. 2:20. [2] Acts 2:17. [3] Mk. 8:38. [4] Rom. 12:1; Rev. 5:8, 10; 1 Pet. 2:9; Rev. 1:6. [5] 1 Tim. 1:18–19. [6] 2 Tim. 2:12; *Eph. 6:12; *Rev. 3:21.

Lord's Day 13

33. Why is He called God's "only begotten Son," since we also are the children of God?

Because Christ alone is the eternal, natural Son of God,[1] but we are children of God by adoption, through grace, for His sake.[2]

[1] Jn. 1:14, 18. [2] Rom. 8:15–17; Eph. 1:5–6; *1 Jn. 3:1.

34. Why do you call Him "our Lord"?

Because not with silver or gold, but with His precious blood, He has redeemed and purchased us, body and soul, from sin and from all the power of the devil, to be His own.[1]

[1] 1 Pet. 1:18–19; 2:9; 1 Cor. 6:20; 7:23; *Acts 2:36; *Tit. 2:14; *Col. 1:14.

Lord's Day 14

35. What is the meaning of "conceived by the Holy Spirit, born of the virgin Mary?"

That the eternal Son of God, who is[1] and continues true and eternal God,[2] took upon Himself the very nature of man, of the flesh and blood of the virgin Mary,[3] by the operation of the Holy Spirit;[4] so that He might also be the true seed of David,[5] like unto His brethren in all things,[6] except for sin.[7]

[1] Jn. 1:1; Rom. 1:3–4. [2] Rom. 9:5. [3] Gal. 4:4; Jn. 1:14. [4] Matt. 1:18–20; Lk. 1:35. [5] Ps. 132:11. [6] Phil. 2:7. [7] Heb. 4:15; *1 Jn. 5:20.

36. What benefit do you receive from the holy conception and birth of Christ?

That He is our Mediator,[1] and with His innocence and perfect holiness covers, in the sight of God, my sin, wherein I was conceived.[2]

[1] Heb. 2:16–17. [2] Ps. 32:1; *1 Jn. 1:9.

Lord's Day 15

37. What do you understand by the word "suffered"?

That all the time He lived on earth, but especially at the end of His life, He bore, in body and soul, the wrath of God against the sin of the whole human race;[1] in order that by His suffering, as the only atoning sacrifice,[2] He might redeem our body and soul from everlasting damnation, and obtain for us the grace of God, righteousness, and eternal life.

[1] 1 Pet. 2:24; Isa. 53:12. [2] 1 Jn. 2:2; 4:10; Rom. 3:25–26; *Ps. 22:14–16; *Matt. 26:38; *Rom. 5:6.

38. Why did He suffer "under Pontius Pilate" as judge?

That He, being innocent, might be condemned by the temporal judge,[1] and thereby deliver us from the severe judgment of God, to which we were exposed.[2]

[1] Acts 4:27–28; Lk. 23:13–15; Jn. 19:4. [2] Ps. 69:4; 2 Cor. 5:21; *Matt. 27:24.

39. Is there anything more in His having been "crucified" than if He had suffered some other death?

Yes, for thereby I am assured that He took upon Himself the curse which lay upon me,[1] because the death of the cross was accursed of God.[2]

[1] Gal. 3:13–14. [2] Deut. 21:22–23; *Phil. 2:8.

Lord's Day 16

40. Why was it necessary for Christ to suffer "death"?

Because the justice and truth[1] of God required that satisfaction for our sins could be made in no other way than by the death of the Son of God.[2]

[1] Gen. 2:17. [2] Heb. 2:9; *Rom. 6:23.

41. Why was He "buried"?

To show thereby that He was really dead.[1]

[1] Matt. 27:59–60; Jn. 19:38–42; Acts 13:29.

42. Since, then, Christ died for us, why must we also die?

Our death is not a satisfaction for our sin, but only a dying to sin and an entering into eternal life.[1]

[1] Jn. 5:24; Phil. 1:23; Rom. 7:24–25.

43. What further benefit do we receive from the sacrifice and death of Christ on the cross?

That by His power our old man is with Him crucified, slain, and buried;[1] so that the evil lusts of the flesh may no more reign in us,[2] but that we may offer ourselves unto Him a sacrifice of thanksgiving.[3]

[1] Rom. 6:6–8; Col. 2:12. [2] Rom. 6:12. [3] Rom. 12:1; *2 Cor. 5:15.

44. Why is it added: "He descended into hell"?

That in my greatest temptations I may be assured that Christ my Lord, by His inexpressible anguish, pains, and terrors, which He suffered in His soul on the cross and before, has redeemed me from the anguish and torment of hell.[1]

[1] Isa. 53:10; Matt. 27:46; *Ps. 18:5; 116:3.

LORD'S DAY 17

45. What benefit do we receive from the "resurrection" of Christ?

First, by His resurrection He has overcome death, that He might make us partakers of the righteousness which He has obtained for us by His death.[1] Second, by His power we are also now raised up to a new life.[2] Third, the resurrection of Christ is to us a sure pledge of our blessed resurrection.[3]

[1] 1 Cor. 15:15,17, 54–55. Rom. 4:25; 1 Pet. 1:3–4, 21. [2] Rom. 6:4; Col. 3:1–4; Eph. 2:5. [3] 1 Cor. 15:12; Rom. 8:11; *1 Cor. 15:20–21.

46. What do you understand by the words "He ascended into heaven"?

That Christ, in the sight of His disciples, was taken up from the earth into heaven,[1] and continues there in our behalf[2] until He shall come again to judge the living and the dead.[3]

[1] Acts 1:9; Matt. 26:64; Mk. 16:19; Lk. 24:51. [2] Heb. 4:14; 7:24–25; 9:11; Rom. 8:34. Eph. 4:10. [3] Acts 1:11; Matt. 24:30; *Acts 3:20–21.

47. But is not Christ with us even unto the end of the world, as He has promised?[1]

Christ is true man and true God. According to His human nature He is now not on earth,[2] but according to His Godhead, majesty, grace, and Spirit, He is at no time absent from us.[3]

[1] Matt. 28:20. [2] Matt. 26:11; Jn. 16:28; 17:11. [3] Jn. 14:17–18; 16:13; Eph. 4:8; Matt. 18:20; *Heb. 8:4.

48. But are not, in this way, the two natures in Christ separated from one another, if the manhood is not wherever the Godhead is?

Not at all, for since the Godhead is incomprehensible and everywhere present,[1] it must follow that the same is not limited with the human nature He assumed, and yet remains personally united to it.[2]

[1] Acts 7:49; Jer. 23:24. [2] Col. 2:9; Jn. 3:13; 11:15; Matt. 28:6; *Jn. 1:48.

Lord's Day 18

49. What benefit do we receive from Christ's ascension into heaven?

First, that He is our Advocate in the presence of His Father in heaven.[1] Second, that we have our flesh in heaven as a sure pledge, that He as the Head, will also take us, His members, up to Himself.[2] Third, that He sends us His Spirit as an earnest,[3] by whose power we seek those things which are above, where Christ sits at the right hand of God, and not things on the earth.[4]

[1] 1 Jn. 2:1; Rom. 8:34. [2] Jn. 14:2; 20:17; Eph. 2:6. [3] Jn. 14:16; Acts 2:33; 2 Cor. 5:5. [4] Col. 3:1; *Jn. 14:3; *Heb. 9:24.

50. Why is it added: "And sits at the right hand of God"?

Because Christ ascended into heaven for this end, that He might there appear as the Head of His Church,[1] by whom the Father governs all things.[2]

[1] Eph. 1:20–23; Col. 1:18. [2] Jn. 5:22; *1 Pet. 3:22; *Ps. 110:1.

Lord's Day 19

51. What does this glory of Christ, our Head, profit us?

First, that by His Holy Spirit He pours out heavenly gifts upon us, His members;[1] then, that by His power He defends and preserves us against all enemies.[2]

[1] Eph. 4:10–12. [2] Ps. 2:9; Jn. 10:28–30; *1 Cor. 15:25–26; *Acts 2:33.

52. What comfort is it to you that Christ "shall come to judge the living and the dead"?

That in all my sorrows and persecutions, I, with uplifted head, look for the very One who offered Himself for me to the judgment of God, and removed all curse from me, to come as Judge from heaven,[1] who shall cast all His and my enemies into everlasting condemnation,[2] but shall take me with all His chosen ones to Himself into heavenly joy and glory.[3]

[1] Lk. 21:28; Rom. 8:23–24; Phil. 3:20–21; Tit. 2:13. [2] 2 Thess. 1:6, 10; 1 Thess. 4:16–18; Matt. 25:41. [3] *Acts 1:10–11; *Heb. 9:28.

God the Holy Spirit

LORD'S DAY 20

53. What do you believe concerning the "Holy Spirit"?

First, that He is co-eternal God with the Father and the Son.[1] Second, that He is also given unto me:[2] by true faith makes me a partaker of Christ and all His benefits,[3] comforts me,[4] and shall abide with me forever.[5]

[1] Gen. 1:2; Isa. 48:16; 1 Cor. 3:16; 6:19; Acts 5:3–4. [2] Matt. 28:19; 2 Cor. 1:21–22. [3] 1 Pet. 1:2; 1 Cor. 6:17. [4] Acts 9:31. [5] Jn. 14:16; 1 Pet. 4:14; *1 Jn. 4:13; *Rom. 15:13.

LORD'S DAY 21

54. What do you believe concerning the "holy, catholic Church"?

That out of the whole human race,[1] from the beginning to the end of the world,[2] the Son of God,[3] by His Spirit and Word,[4] gathers, defends, and preserves for Himself unto everlasting life a chosen communion[5] in the unity of the true faith;[6] and that I am and forever shall remain a living member of this communion.[7]

[1] Gen. 26:4. [2] Jn. 10:10. [3] Eph. 1:10–13. [4] Rom. 1:16; Isa. 59:21; Rom. 10:14–17; Eph. 5:26. [5] Rom. 8:29–30; Matt. 16:18; Eph. 4:3–6. [6] Acts 2:46; Ps. 71:18; 1 Cor. 11:26; Jn. 10:28–30; 1 Cor. 1:8–9. [7] 1 Jn. 3:21; 1 Jn. 2:19; *Gal. 3:28.

55. What do you understand by the "communion of saints"?

First, that believers, one and all, as members of the Lord Jesus Christ, are partakers with Him in all His treasures and gifts;[1] second, that each one must feel himself bound to use his gifts readily and cheerfully for the advantage and welfare of other members.[2]

[1] 1 Jn. 1:3. [2] 1 Cor. 12:12–13, 21; 13:5–6; Phil. 2:4–6; *Heb. 3:14.

56. What do you believe concerning the "forgiveness of sins"?

That God, for the sake of Christ's satisfaction,[1] will no more remember my sins, nor the sinful nature with which I have to struggle all my life long;[2] but graciously imputes to me the righteousness of Christ, that I may nevermore come into condemnation.[3]

[1] 1 Jn. 2:2. [2] 2 Cor. 5:19, 21; Rom. 7:24–25; Ps. 103:3, 10–12; Jer. 31:34; Rom. 8:1–4. [3] Jn. 3:18; *Eph. 1:7; *Rom. 4:7–8; 7:18.

LORD'S DAY 22

57. What comfort do you receive from the "resurrection of the body"?

That not only my soul after this life shall be immediately taken up to Christ its Head,[1] but also that this my body, raised by the power of Christ, shall be reunited with my soul, and made like the glorious body of Christ.[2]

[1] Lk. 23:43; Phil. 1:21–23. [2] 1 Cor. 15:53–54; Job 19:25–27; 1 Jn. 3:2.

58. What comfort do you receive from the article "life everlasting"?

That, inasmuch as I now feel in my heart the beginning of eternal joy,[1] I shall after this life possess complete blessedness, such as eye has not seen, nor ear heard, neither has entered into the heart of man,[2] therein to praise God forever.[3]

[1] 2 Cor. 5:2–3. [2] 1 Cor. 2:9. [3] Jn. 17:3; *Rom. 8:23; *1 Pet. 1:8.

LORD'S DAY 23

59. What does it help you now, that you believe all this?

That I am righteous in Christ before God, and an heir of eternal life.[1]

[1] Hab. 2:4; Rom. 1:17; Jn. 3:36; *Tit. 3:7; *Rom. 5:1; *Rom. 8:16.

60. How are you righteous before God?

Only by true faith in Jesus Christ:[1] that is, although my conscience accuses me, that I have grievously sinned against all the commandments of God, and have never kept any of them,[2] and am still prone always to all evil;[3] yet God, without any merit of mine,[4] of mere grace,[5] grants and imputes to me the perfect satisfaction,[6] righteousness, and holiness of Christ,[7] as if I had never committed nor had any sins, and had myself accomplished all the obedience which Christ has fulfilled for me;[8] if only I accept such benefit with a believing heart.[9]

[1] Rom. 3:21–25; Gal. 2:16; Eph. 2:8–9; Phil. 3:9. [2] Rom. 3:9–10. [3] Rom. 7:23. [4] Tit. 3:5. [5] Rom. 3:24; Eph. 2:8. [6] 1 Jn. 2:2. [7] 1 Jn. 2:1; Rom. 4:4–5; 2 Cor. 5:19. [8] 2 Cor. 5:21. [9] Jn. 3:18; *Rom. 3:28; *Rom. 10:10.

61. Why do you say that you are righteous by faith only?

Not that I am acceptable to God on account of the worthiness of my faith, but because only the satisfaction, righteousness, and holiness of Christ is my righteousness before God;[1] and I can receive the same and make it my own in no other way than by faith only.[2]

[1] 1 Cor. 1:30; 2:2. [2] 1 Jn. 5:10. *Isa. 53:5; *Gal. 3:22; *Rom. 4:16.

LORD'S DAY 24

62. But why cannot our good works be the whole or part of our righteousness before God?

Because the righteousness which can stand before the judgment seat of God must be perfect throughout and entirely conformable to the divine law,[1] but even our best works in this life are all imperfect and defiled with sin.[2]

[1] Gal. 3:10; Deut. 27:26. [2] Isa. 64:6; *Jas. 2:10; *Phil. 3:12.

63. Do our good works merit nothing, even though it is God's will to reward them in this life and in that which is to come?

The reward comes not of merit, but of grace.[1]

[1] Lk. 17:10; *Rom. 11:6.

64. But does not this doctrine make men careless and profane?

No, for it is impossible that those who are implanted into Christ by true faith, should not bring forth fruits of thankfulness.[1]

[1] Matt. 7:18; *Rom. 6:1–2; *Jn. 15:5.

The Sacraments

LORD'S DAY 25

65. Since, then, we are made partakers of Christ and all His benefits by faith only, where does this faith come from?

The Holy Spirit works faith in our hearts[1] by the preaching of the Holy Gospel, and confirms it by the use of the holy sacraments.[2]

[1] Jn. 3:5; *Rom. 10:17. [2] Rom. 4:11; *Acts 8:37.

66. What are the sacraments?

The sacraments are visible holy signs and seals appointed by God for this end, that by their use He may the more fully declare and seal to us the promise of the Gospel, namely, that of free grace He grants us the forgiveness of sins and everlasting life for the sake of the one sacrifice of Christ accomplished on the cross.[1]

[1] Gen. 17:11; Rom. 4:11; Deut. 30:6; Heb. 9:8–9; Ezek. 20:12.

67. **Are both the Word and the sacraments designed to direct our faith to the sacrifice of Christ on the cross as the only ground of our salvation?**

Yes, truly, for the Holy Spirit teaches in the Gospel and assures us by the holy sacraments, that our whole salvation stands in the one sacrifice of Christ made for us on the cross.[1]

[1] Rom. 6:3; *Gal. 3:27; *Heb. 9:12; *Acts 2:41–42.

68. **How many sacraments has Christ instituted in the New Testament?**

Two: Holy Baptism and the Holy Supper.

Holy Baptism

Lord's Day 26

69. **How is it signified and sealed to you in Holy Baptism that you have part in the one sacrifice of Christ on the cross?**

Thus: that Christ instituted this outward washing with water[1] and joined to it this promise,[2] that I am washed with His blood and Spirit from the pollution of my soul, that is, from all my sins, as certainly as I am washed outwardly with water, whereby commonly the filthiness of the body is taken away.[3]

[1] Matt. 28:19–20; Acts 2:38. [2] Matt. 3:11; Mk. 16:16; Rom. 6:3–4. [3] Mk. 1:4.

70. **What is it to be washed with the blood and Spirit of Christ?**

It is to have the forgiveness of sins from God through grace, for the sake of Christ's blood, which He shed for us in His sacrifice on the cross;[1] and also to be renewed by the Holy Spirit and sanctified to be members of Christ, so that we may more and more die unto sin and lead holy and blameless lives.[2]

[1] Heb. 12:24; 1 Pet. 1:2; Rev. 1:5; Zech. 13:1; Ezek. 36:25–27. [2] Jn. 1:33; 3:3; 1 Cor. 6:11; 12:13; *Heb. 9:14.

71. **Where has Christ promised that we are as certainly washed with His blood and Spirit as with the water of Baptism?**

In the institution of Baptism, which says, "Go therefore and make disciples of all the nations, baptizing them in the name of the Father and of the Son and of the Holy Spirit."[1] "He who believes and is baptized will be saved; but he who does not believe will be condemned."[2] This promise is also repeated where Scripture calls Baptism the washing of regeneration[3] and the washing away of sins.[4]

[1] Matt. 28:19 [2] Mk. 16:16. [3] Tit. 3:5. [4] Acts 22:16.

Lord's Day 27

72. Is, then, the outward washing with water itself the washing away of sins?

No,[1] for only the blood of Jesus Christ and the Holy Spirit cleanse us from all sin.[2]

[1] 1 Pet. 3:21; Eph. 5:26. [2] 1 Jn. 1:7; 1 Cor. 6:11.

73. Why then does the Holy Spirit call Baptism the washing of regeneration and the washing away of sins?

God speaks thus with great cause, namely, not only to teach us thereby that just as the filthiness of the body is taken away by water, so our sins are taken away by the blood and Spirit of Christ;[1] but much more, that by this divine pledge and token He may assure us that we are as really washed from our sins spiritually as our bodies are washed with water.[2]

[1] Rev. 7:14. [2] Mk. 16:16; *Acts 2:38.

74. Are infants also to be baptized?

Yes, for since they, as well as their parents, belong to the covenant and people of God,[1] and through the blood of Christ[2] both redemption from sin and the Holy Spirit, who works faith, are promised to them no less than to their parents,[3] they are also by Baptism, as a sign of the covenant, to be engrafted into the Christian Church, and distinguished from the children of unbelievers,[4] as was done in the Old Testament by circumcision,[5] in place of which in the New Testament Baptism is appointed.[6]

[1] Gen. 17:7. [2] Matt. 19:14. [3] Lk. 1:14–15; Ps. 22:10; Acts 2:39. [4] Acts 10:47 [5] Gen. 17:14. [6] Col. 2:11–13.

The Holy Supper

Lord's Day 28

75. How is it signified and sealed to you in the Holy Supper that you partake of the one sacrifice of Christ on the cross and all His benefits?

Thus: that Christ has commanded me and all believers to eat of this broken bread and to drink of this cup in remembrance of Him, and has joined therewith these promises:[1] first, that His body was offered and broken on the cross for me and His blood shed for me, as certainly as I see with my eyes the bread of the Lord broken for me and the cup communicated to me; and further, that with His crucified body and shed blood He Himself feeds and nourishes my soul to everlasting life, as certainly as I receive from the hand of the minister and taste with my mouth the bread and cup of the Lord, which are given me as certain tokens of the body and blood of Christ.

[1] Matt. 26:26–28; Mk. 14:22–24; Lk. 22:19–20; 1 Cor. 10:16–17; 11:23–25; 12:13.

76. What does it mean to eat the crucified body and drink the shed blood of Christ?

It means not only to embrace with a believing heart all the sufferings and death of Christ, and thereby to obtain the forgiveness of sins and life eternal;[1] but moreover, also, to be so united more and more to His sacred body by the Holy Spirit,[2] who dwells both in Christ and in us, that, although He is in heaven[3] and we on earth, we are nevertheless flesh of His flesh and bone of His bone,[4] and live and are governed forever by one Spirit, as members of the same body are governed by one soul.[5]

[1] Jn. 6:35, 40, 47–48, 50–54. [2] Jn. 6:55–56. [3] Acts 3:21; 1 Cor. 11:26. [4] Eph. 3:16–19; 5:29–30, 32; 1 Cor. 6:15, 17, 19; 1 Jn. 4:13. [5] Jn.14:23; Jn. 6:56–58; Jn. 15:1–6; Eph. 4:15–16; Jn. 6:63.

77. Where has Christ promised that He will thus feed and nourish believers with His body and blood as certainly as they eat of this broken bread and drink of this cup?

In the institution of the Supper, which says: "The Lord Jesus on the same night in which He was betrayed took bread; and when He had given thanks, He broke it and said, 'Take, eat; this is My body which is broken for you; do this in remembrance of Me.' In the same manner He also took the cup after supper, saying, 'This cup is the new covenant in My blood. This do, as often as you drink it, in remembrance of Me.' For as often as you eat this bread and drink this cup, you proclaim the Lord's death till He comes."[1]

And this promise is also repeated by the Apostle Paul, where he says, "The cup of blessing which we bless, is it not the communion of the blood of Christ? The bread which we break, is it not the communion of the body of Christ? Because there is one bread, so we being many are one body, for we are all partakers of that one bread."[2]

[1] 1 Cor. 11:23-26. [2] 1 Cor. 10:16–17.

Lord's Day 29

78. **Do, then, the bread and the wine become the real body and blood of Christ?**

No, but as the water in Baptism is not changed into the blood of Christ, nor becomes the washing away of sins itself, being only the divine token and assurance thereof,[1] so also in the Lord's Supper the sacred bread[2] does not become the body of Christ itself, though agreeably to the nature and usage of sacraments it is called the body of Christ.[3]

[1] Matt. 26:29. [2] 1 Cor. 11:26–28. [3] Ex. 12:26–27, 43, 48; 1 Cor. 10:1–4.

79. **Why then does Christ call the bread His body, and the cup His blood, or the new testament in His blood; and the Apostle Paul, the communion of the body and the blood of Christ?**

Christ speaks thus with great cause, namely, not only to teach us thereby, that like as the bread and wine sustain this temporal life, so also His crucified body and shed blood are the true meat and drink of our souls unto life eternal;[1] but much more, by this visible sign and pledge to assure us that we are as really partakers of His true body and blood by the working of the Holy Spirit, as we receive by the mouth of the body these holy tokens in remembrance of Him;[2] and that all His sufferings and obedience are as certainly our own, as if we ourselves had suffered and done all in our own person.

[1] Jn. 6:51–55 (See Question 76). [2] 1 Cor. 10:16–17 (See Question 78).

Lord's Day 30

80. **What difference is there between the Lord's Supper and the Pope's Mass?**

The Lord's Supper testifies to us that we have full forgiveness of all our sins by the one sacrifice of Jesus Christ, which He Himself once accomplished on the cross;[1] and that by the Holy Spirit we are engrafted into Christ,[2] who, with His true body is now in heaven at the right hand of the Father,[3] and is there to be worshiped.[4] But the Mass teaches that the living and the dead do not have forgiveness of sins through the sufferings of Christ, unless Christ is still daily offered for them by the priests, and that Christ is bodily under the form of bread and wine, and is therefore to be worshiped in them. And thus the Mass at bottom is nothing else than a denial of the one sacrifice and suffering of Jesus Christ,[5] and an accursed idolatry.

[1] Heb. 7:27; 9:12, 25–28; 10:10, 12, 14; Jn. 19:30. [2] 1 Cor. 6:17. [3] Heb. 1:3; 8:1. [4] Jn. 4:21–24; 20:17; Lk. 24:52; Acts 7:55; Col. 3:1; Phil. 3:20–21; 1 Thess. 1:9–10. [5] See Hebrews chapters 9 and 10; *Matt. 4:10.

81. Who are to come to the table of the Lord?

Those who are displeased with themselves for their sins, yet trust that these are forgiven them, and that their remaining infirmity is covered by the suffering and death of Christ; who also desire more and more to strengthen their faith and to amend their life. But the unrepentant and hypocrites eat and drink judgment to themselves.[1]

[1] 1 Cor. 10:19–22; 11:28–29; *Ps. 51:3; *Jn. 7:37–38; Ps. 103:1–4; *Matt. 5:6.

82. Are they, then, also to be admitted to this Supper who show themselves by their confession and life to be unbelieving and ungodly?

No, for thereby the covenant of God is profaned and His wrath provoked against the whole congregation;[1] therefore, the Christian Church is bound, according to the order of Christ and His Apostles, to exclude such persons by the Office of the Keys until they amend their lives.

[1] 1 Cor. 11:20, 34a; Isa. 1:11–15; 66:3; Jer. 7:21–23; Ps. 50:16–17; *Matt. 7:6; *1 Cor. 11:30–32; *Tit. 3:10–11; *2 Thess. 3:6.

Lord's Day 31

83. What is the Office of the Keys?

The preaching of the Holy Gospel and Christian discipline; by these two the kingdom of heaven is opened to believers and shut against unbelievers.[1]

[1] Matt. 16:18–19; 18:18; *Jn. 20:23; *Lk. 24:46–47; *1 Cor. 1:23–24.

84. How is the kingdom of heaven opened and shut by the preaching of the Holy Gospel?

In this way: that, according to the command of Christ, it is proclaimed and openly witnessed to believers, one and all, that as often as they accept with true faith the promise of the Gospel, all their sins are really forgiven them of God for the sake of Christ's merits; and on the contrary, to all unbelievers and hypocrites, that the wrath of God and eternal condemnation abide on them so long as they are not converted.[1] According to this testimony of the Gospel, God will judge men both in this life and in that which is to come.

[1] Jn. 20:21–23; *Acts 10:43; *Isa. 58:1; *2 Cor. 2:15–16; *Jn. 8:24.

85. How is the kingdom of heaven shut and opened by Christian discipline?

In this way: that, according to the command of Christ, if any under the Christian name show themselves unsound either in doctrine or in life, and after several brotherly admonitions do not turn from their errors or evil ways, they are complained of to the Church or to its proper officers; and, if they neglect to hear them also, are by them denied the holy sacraments and thereby excluded from the Christian communion, and by God Himself from the kingdom of Christ; and if they promise and show real amendment, they are again received as members of Christ and His Church.[1]

[1] Matt. 18:15–18; 1 Cor. 5:3–5, 11; 2 Thess. 3:14–15; 2 Jn. 1:10–11.

THIRD PART: THANKFULNESS

LORD'S DAY 32

86. Since, then, we are redeemed from our misery by grace through Christ, without any merit of ours, why must we do good works?

Because Christ, having redeemed us by His blood, also renews us by His Holy Spirit after His own image, that with our whole life we show ourselves thankful to God for His blessing,[1] and that He be glorified through us;[2] then also, that we ourselves may be assured of our faith by the fruits thereof;[3] and by our godly walk win also others to Christ.[4]

[1] Rom. 6:13; 12:1–2; 1 Pet. 2:5, 9–10; 1 Cor. 6:20. [2] Matt. 5:16; 1 Pet. 2:12. [3] Matt. 7:17–18; Gal. 5:6, 22–23. [4] Rom. 14:19; 1 Pet. 3:1–2; *2 Pet. 1:10.

87. Can they, then, not be saved who do not turn to God from their unthankful, unrepentant life?

By no means, for, as Scripture says, no unchaste person, idolater, adulterer, thief, covetous man, drunkard, slanderer, robber, or the like shall inherit the kingdom of God.[1]

[1] 1 Cor. 6:9–10; Eph. 5:5–6; 1 Jn. 3:14–15.

LORD'S DAY 33

88. In how many things does true repentance or conversion consist?

In two things: the dying of the old man,[1] and the making alive of the new.

[1] Rom. 6:4–6; Eph. 4:22–24; Col. 3:5–10; 1 Cor. 5:7.

89. What is the dying of the old man?

Heartfelt sorrow for sin, causing us to hate and turn from it always more and more.[1]

[1] Rom. 8:13; Joel 2:13.

90. What is the making alive of the new man?

Heartfelt joy in God through Christ,[1] causing us to take delight in living according to the will of God in all good works.[2]

[1] Rom. 5:1; 14:17; Isa. 57:15. [2] Rom. 8:10–11; Gal. 2:20; *Rom. 7:22.

91. What are good works?

Those only which proceed from true faith,[1] and are done according to the law of God,[2] unto His glory,[3] and not such as rest on our own opinion[4] or the commandments of men.[5]

[1] Rom. 14:23. [2] 1 Sam. 15:22; Eph. 2:10. [3] 1 Cor. 10:31. [4] Deut. 12:32; Ezek. 20:18, 20; Isa. 29:13. [5] Matt. 15:9; *Num. 15:39.

The Law of God

92. What is the law of God?

"And God spoke all these words, saying:"

First Commandment

"I am the Lord your God, who brought you out of the land of Egypt, out of the house of bondage. You shall have no other gods before Me."

Second Commandment

"You shall not make for yourself a carved image—any likeness of anything that is in heaven above, or that is in the earth beneath, or that is in the water under the earth; you shall not bow down to them nor serve them. For I, the Lord your God, am a jealous God, visiting the iniquity of the fathers upon the children to the third and fourth generations of those who hate Me, but showing mercy to thousands, to those who love Me and keep My commandments."

Third Commandment

"You shall not take the name of the Lord your God in vain, for the Lord will not hold him guiltless who takes His name in vain."

Fourth Commandment

"Remember the Sabbath day, to keep it holy. Six days you shall labor and do all your work, but the seventh day is the Sabbath of the Lord your God. In it you shall do no work: you, nor your son, nor your daughter, nor your male servant, nor your female servant, nor your cattle, nor your stranger who is within your gates. For in six days the Lord made the heavens and the earth, the sea, and all that is in them, and rested the seventh day. Therefore the Lord blessed the Sabbath day and hallowed it."

Fifth Commandment

"Honor your father and your mother, that your days may be long upon the land which the Lord your God is giving you."

Sixth Commandment

"You shall not murder."

Seventh Commandment

"You shall not commit adultery."

Eighth Commandment

"You shall not steal."

Ninth Commandment

"You shall not bear false witness against your neighbor."

Tenth Commandment

"You shall not covet your neighbor's house; you shall not covet your neighbor's wife, nor his male servant, nor his female servant, nor his ox, nor his donkey, nor anything that is your neighbor's."[1]

[1] Ex. 20; Deut. 5; *Matt. 5:17–19; *Rom. 10:5; *Rom. 3:31; *Ps. 119:9.

Lord's Day 34

93. How are these commandments divided?

Into two tables:[1] the first of which teaches, in four commandments, what duties we owe to God; the second, in six, what duties we owe to our neighbor.[2]

[1] Ex. 34:28; Deut. 4:13. [2] Matt. 22:37–40.

94. What does God require in the first commandment?

That, on peril of my soul's salvation, I avoid and flee all idolatry,[1] sorcery, enchantments,[2] invocation of saints or of other creatures;[3] and that I rightly acknowledge the only true God,[4] trust in Him alone,[5] with all humility [6] and patience[7] expect all good from Him only,[8] and love,[9] fear,[10] and honor[11] Him with my whole heart; so as rather to renounce all creatures than to do the least thing against His will.[12]

[1] 1 Cor. 10:7, 14. [2] Lev. 19:31; Deut. 18:10–12. [3] Matt. 4:10; Rev. 19:10; 22:8–9. [4] Jn. 17:3. [5] Jer. 17:5. [6] 1 Pet. 5:5–6. [7] Heb. 10:36; Col. 1:10b–11; Rom. 5:3–4; 1 Cor. 10:10. [8] Ps. 104:27–30; Isa. 45:6b–7; Jas. 1:17. [9] Deut. 6:5. [10] Deut. 6:2; Ps. 111:10; Prov. 9:10; Matt. 10:28. [11] Deut. 10:20. [12] Matt. 5:29–30; 10:37; Acts 5:29.

95. What is idolatry?

Idolatry is to conceive or have something else in which to place our trust instead of, or besides, the one true God who has revealed Himself in His Word.[1]

[1] Eph. 5:5; Phil. 3:19; Eph. 2:12; Jn. 2:23; 2 Jn. 1:9; Jn. 5:23; *Ps. 81:8–9; *Matt. 6:24; Ps. 62:5–7 *Ps. 73:25–26.

LORD'S DAY 35

96. What does God require in the second commandment?

That we in no way make any image of God,[1] nor worship Him in any other way than He has commanded us in His Word.[2]

[1] Deut. 4:15–19; Isa. 40:18, 25. Rom. 1:22–24; Acts 17:29. [2] 1 Sam. 15:23; Deut. 12:30–32; Matt. 15:9; *Deut. 4:23–24; *Jn. 4:24.

97. May we not make any image at all?

God may not and cannot be imaged in any way; as for creatures, though they may indeed be imaged, yet God forbids the making or keeping of any likeness of them, either to worship them or to serve God by them.[1]

[1] Ex. 23:24–25; 34:13–14; Deut. 7:5; 12:3; 16:22; 2 Kgs. 18:4; *Jn. 1:18.

98. But may not pictures be tolerated in churches as books for the people?

No, for we should not be wiser than God, who will not have His people taught by dumb idols,[1] but by the lively preaching of His Word.[2]

[1] Jer. 10:8; Hab. 2:18–19. [2] 2 Pet. 1:19; 2 Tim. 3:16–17; Rom. 10:17.

LORD'S DAY 36

99. What is required in the third commandment?

That we must not by cursing,[1] or by false swearing,[2] nor yet by unnecessary oaths,[3] profane or abuse the name of God; nor even by our silence and connivance be partakers of these horrible sins in others; and in summary, that we use the holy name of God in no other way than with fear and reverence,[4] so that He may be rightly confessed[5] and worshiped[6] by us, and be glorified in all our words and works.[7]

[1] Lev. 24:10–16. [2] Lev. 19:12. [3] Matt. 5:37; Jas. 5:12. [4] Isa. 45:23. [5] Matt. 10:32. [6] 1 Tim. 2:8. [7] Rom. 2:24; 1 Tim. 6:1; Col. 3:16–17; *1 Pet. 3:15.

100. Is the profaning of God's name, by swearing and cursing, so grievous a sin that His wrath is kindled against those also who do not help as much as they can to hinder and forbid it?

Yes, truly,[1] for no sin is greater and more provoking to God than the profaning of His name; wherefore He even commanded it to be punished with death.[2]

[1] Lev. 5:1 [2] Lev. 24:15–16; *Lev. 19:12; *Prov. 29:24–25.

LORD'S DAY 37

101. But may we swear reverently by the name of God?

Yes, when the magistrate requires it, or when it may be needful otherwise, to maintain and promote fidelity and truth to the glory of God and our neighbor's good; for such an oath is grounded in God's Word,[1] and therefore was rightly used by the saints in the Old and New Testaments.[2]

[1] Deut. 10:20; Isa. 48:1; Heb. 6:16. [2] Gen. 21:24; 31:53–54; Josh. 9:15, 19; 1 Sam. 24:22; 1 Kgs. 1:29; Rom. 1:9.

102. May we swear by "the saints" or by any other creatures?

No, for a lawful oath is a calling upon God, that He, as the only searcher of hearts, may bear witness to the truth, and punish me if I swear falsely;[1] which honor is due to no creature.[2]

[1] 2 Cor. 1:23. [2] Matt. 5:34–36; *Jer. 5:7; *Isa. 65:16.

LORD'S DAY 38

103. What does God require in the fourth commandment?

In the first place, God wills that the ministry of the Gospel and schools be maintained,[1] and that I, especially on the day of rest, diligently attend church[2] to learn the Word of God,[3] to use the holy sacraments,[4] to call publicly upon the Lord,[5] and to give Christian alms.[6] In the second place, that all the days of my life I rest from my evil works, allow the Lord to work in me by His Spirit, and thus begin in this life the everlasting Sabbath.[7]

[1] Tit. 1:5; 1 Tim. 3:14–15; 4:13–14; 5:17; 1 Cor. 9:11, 13–14. [2] 2 Tim. 2:2, 15; Ps. 40:10–11; 68:26; Acts 2:42, 46. [3] 1 Cor. 14:19, 29, 31. [4] 1 Cor. 11:33. [5] 1 Tim. 2:1–2, 8–10; 1 Cor. 14:16. [6] 1 Cor. 16:2. [7] Isa. 66:23; *Gal. 6:6; *Acts 20:7; Heb. 4:9–10.

Lord's Day 39

104. What does God require in the fifth commandment?

That I show all honor, love, and faithfulness to my father and mother,[1] and to all in authority over me,[2] submit myself with due obedience to all their good instruction and correction, and also bear patiently with their infirmities, since it is God's will to govern us by their hand.[3]

[1] Eph. 6:22; Eph. 6:1–6; Col. 3:18, 20–24; Prov. 1:8–9; 4:1; 15:20; 20:20; Ex. 21:17; Gen. 9:24–25. [2] Rom. 13:1; 1 Pet. 2:18; Rom. 13:2–7; Matt. 22:21. [3] Eph. 6:4, 9; Col. 3:19, 21; *Prov. 30:17; *Deut. 27:16; *Deut. 32:24; *Prov. 13:24; *1 Tim. 2:1–2; *1 Tim. 5:17; *Heb. 13:17–18.

Lord's Day 40

105. What does God require in the sixth commandment?

That I do not revile, hate, insult, or kill my neighbor either in thought, word, or gesture, much less in deed, whether by myself or by another,[1] but lay aside all desire of revenge;[2] moreover, that I do not harm myself, nor willfully run into any danger.[3] Wherefore also to restrain murder the magistrate is armed with the sword.[4]

[1] Matt. 5:21–22; 26:52; Gen. 9:6. [2] Eph. 4:26; Rom. 1:19; Matt. 5:25; 18:35. [3] Matt. 4:7; Rom. 13:14; Col. 2:23. [4] Ex. 21:14; *Matt. 18:6–7.

106. Does this commandment speak only of killing?

No, but in forbidding murder God teaches us that He abhors its very root, namely, envy,[1] hatred,[2] anger,[3] and desire of revenge; and that in His sight all these are hidden murder.[4]

[1] Rom. 1:28–32. [2] 1 Jn. 2:9–11. [3] Jas. 2:13; Gal. 5:19–21. [4] 1 Jn. 3:15 *Jas. 3:16; *1:19.

107. But is this all that is required: that we do not kill our neighbor?

No, for in condemning envy, hatred, and anger, God requires us to love our neighbor as ourselves,[1] to show patience, peace, meekness,[2] mercy,[3] and kindness[4] toward him, and to prevent his hurt as much as possible;[5] also, to do good even unto our enemies.[6]

[1] Matt. 7:12; 22:39. [2] Eph. 4:2; Gal. 6:1–2; Rom. 12:18. [3] Matt. 5:7; Lk. 6:36. [4] Rom. 12:10. [5] Ex. 23:5. [6] Matt. 5:44–45; Rom. 12:20–21; *Col. 3:12–14; *Matt. 5:9.

Lord's Day 41

108. What does the seventh commandment teach us?

That all unchastity is accursed of God,[1] and that we should therefore loathe it with our whole heart,[2] and live chastely and modestly,[3] whether in holy wedlock or single life.[4]

[1] Lev. 18:27–28. [2] Jude 1:22–23. [3] 1 Thess. 4:3–5. [4] Heb. 13:4; 1 Cor. 7:1–4.

109. Does God forbid nothing more in this commandment than adultery and such gross sins?

Since both our body and soul are temples of the Holy Spirit, it is His will that we keep both pure and holy; therefore, He forbids all unchaste actions, gestures, words,[1] thoughts, desires,[2] and whatever may entice thereto.[3]

[1] Eph. 5:3–4; 1 Cor. 6:18–20. [2] Matt. 5:27–30. [3] Eph. 5:18–19; 1 Cor. 15:33.

Lord's Day 42

110. What does God forbid in the eighth commandment?

God forbids not only such theft[1] and robbery[2] as are punished by the government, but God views as theft also all wicked tricks and devices, whereby we seek to get our neighbor's goods, whether by force or by deceit,[3] such as unjust weights,[4] lengths, measures,[5] goods, coins, usury,[6] or by any means forbidden of God; also all covetousness[7] and the misuse and waste of His gifts.[8]

[1] 1 Cor. 6:10. [2] 1 Cor. 5:10. [3] Lk. 3:14; 1 Thess. 4:6. [4] Prov. 11:1; 16:11. [5] Ezek. 45:9–10. Deut. 25:13–15. [6] Ps. 15:5; Lk. 6:35. [7] 1 Cor. 6:10. [8] Prov. 5:10; *1 Tim. 6:10; *Jn. 6:12.

111. But what does God require of you in this commandment?

That I further my neighbor's good where I can and may, deal with him as I would have others deal with me,[1] and labor faithfully, so that I may be able to help the poor in their need.[2]

[1] Matt. 7:12. [2] Eph. 4:28; *Phil. 2:4; *Gen. 3:19; *1 Tim. 6:6–7.

LORD'S DAY 43

112. What does the ninth commandment require?

That I bear false witness against no one,[1] twist no one's words,[2] be no backbiter or slanderer,[3] join in condemning no one unheard or rashly;[4] but that on pain of God's heavy wrath, I avoid all lying and deceit[5] as the very works of the devil;[6] and that in matters of judgment and justice and in all other affairs, I love, speak honestly, and confess the truth;[7] also, insofar as I can, defend and promote my neighbor's good name.[8]

[1] Prov. 19:5, 9. [2] Ps. 15:3. [3] Rom. 1:28–30. [4] Matt. 7:1–2. Lk. 6:37. [5] Jn. 8:44. [6] Prov. 12:22; 13:5. [7] 1 Cor. 13:6; Eph. 4:25. [8] 1 Pet. 4:8; *Jn. 7:24, 51; *1 Pet. 2:21, 23; *Col. 4:6; *1 Pet 3:9.

LORD'S DAY 44

113. What does the tenth commandment require?

That not even the least inclination or thought against any commandment of God ever enter our heart, but that with our whole heart we continually hate all sin and take pleasure in all righteousness.[1]

[1] Rom. 7:7–8; *Prov. 4:23; *Jas. 1:14–15; *Matt. 15:11, 19–20.

114. Can those who are converted to God keep these commandments perfectly?

No, but even the holiest men, while in this life, have only a small beginning of such obedience,[1] yet so that with earnest purpose they begin to live not only according to some, but according to all the commandments of God.[2]

[1] 1 Jn. 1:8–10; Rom. 7:14–15; Eccl. 7:20. [2] Rom. 7:22; Jas. 2:10–11; *Job 9:2–3; *Ps. 19:13.

115. Why then does God so strictly enjoin the Ten Commandments upon us, since in this life no one can keep them?

First, that as long as we live we may learn more and more to know our sinful nature,[1] and so the more earnestly seek forgiveness of sins and righteousness in Christ;[2] second, that without ceasing we diligently ask God for the grace of the Holy Spirit, that we be renewed more and more after the image of God, until we attain the goal of perfection after this life.[3]

[1] 1 Jn. 1:9; Ps. 32:5. [2] Rom. 7:24–25. [3] 1 Cor. 9:24–25; Phil. 3:12–14; *Matt. 5:6; *Ps. 51:12.

Prayer

LORD'S DAY 45

116. Why is prayer necessary for Christians?

Because it is the chief part of thankfulness which God requires of us,[1] and because God will give His grace and Holy Spirit only to those who earnestly and without ceasing ask them of Him, and render thanks unto Him for them.[2]

[1] Ps. 50:14–15. [2] Matt. 7:7–8; Lk. 11:9–10, 13; Matt. 13:12; *Eph. 6:18.

117. What belongs to such prayer which is acceptable to God and which He will hear?

First, that with our whole heart[1] we call only upon the one true God, who has revealed Himself to us in His Word,[2] for all that He has commanded us to ask of Him;[3] second, that we thoroughly know our need and misery,[4] so as to humble ourselves in the presence of His divine majesty;[5] third, that we be firmly assured[6] that notwithstanding our unworthiness, He will, for the sake of Christ our Lord, certainly hear our prayer,[7] as He has promised us in His Word.[8]

[1] Jn. 4:22–24. [2] Rom. 8:26; 1 Jn. 5:14. [3] Ps. 27:8. [4] 2 Chron. 20:12. [5] Ps. 2:10; 34:18; Isa. 66:2. [6] Rom. 10:14; Jas. 1:6. [7] Jn. 14:13–16; Dan. 9:17–18. [8] Matt. 7:8; Ps. 143:1; *Lk. 18:13.

118. What has God commanded us to ask of Him?

All things necessary for soul and body,[1] which Christ our Lord comprised in the prayer which He Himself taught us.

[1] Jas. 1:17. Matt. 6:33. *1 Pet. 5:7. *Phil. 4:6.

119. What is the Lord's Prayer?

Our Father in heaven, hallowed be Your name. Your kingdom come. Your will be done on earth as it is in heaven. Give us this day our daily bread. And forgive us our debts, as we forgive our debtors. And do not lead us into temptation, but deliver us from the evil one. For Yours is the kingdom and the power and the glory forever. Amen.[1]

[1] Matt. 6:9–13; Lk. 11:2–4.

Lord's Day 46

120. Why did Christ command us to address God thus: "Our Father"?

To awaken in us at the very beginning of our prayer that childlike reverence for and trust in God, which are to be the ground of our prayer, namely, that God has become our Father through Christ, and will much less deny us what we ask of Him in faith than our parents refuse us earthly things.[1]

[1] Matt. 7:9–11; Lk. 11:11–13; *1 Pet. 1:17; *Isa. 63:16.

121. Why is it added, "in heaven"?

That we might have no earthly thought of the heavenly majesty of God,[1] and from His almighty power expect all things necessary for body and soul.[2]

[1] Jer. 23:23–24; Acts 17:24–25, 27. [2] Rom. 10:12; *1 Kgs. 8:28; *Ps. 115:3.

Lord's Day 47

122. What is the first petition?

"Hallowed be Your name;" that is, grant us, first, rightly to know You,[1] and to sanctify, magnify, and praise You in all Your works, in which Your power, goodness, justice, mercy, and truth shine forth;[2] and further, that we so order our whole life, our thoughts, words, and deeds, that Your Name may not be blasphemed, but honored and praised on our account.[3]

[1] Jn. 17:3; Matt. 16:17; Jas. 1:5; Ps. 119:105. [2] Ps. 119:137; Rom. 11:33–36. [3] Ps. 71:8; *Ps. 100:3–4; *Ps. 92:1–2; *Eph. 1:16–17; *Ps. 71:16.

Lord's Day 48

123. What is the second petition?

"Your kingdom come;" that is, so govern us by Your Word and Spirit, that we submit ourselves to You always more and more;[1] preserve and increase Your Church;[2] destroy the works of the devil, every power that exalts itself against You, and all wicked devices formed against Your Holy Word,[3] until the fullness of Your kingdom come,[4] wherein You shall be all in all.[5]

[1] Ps. 119:5; 143:10. [2] Ps. 51:18; 122:6–7. [3] 1 Jn. 3:8; Rom. 16:20. [4] Rev. 22:17, 20; Rom. 8:22–23. [5] 1 Cor. 15:28; *Ps. 102:12–13; *Heb. 12:28; *Rev. 11:15; *1 Cor. 15:24.

LORD'S DAY 49

124. What is the third petition?

"Your will be done on earth, as it is in heaven;" that is, grant that
we and all men renounce our own will,[1] and without disputing
obey Your will, which alone is good;[2] so that every one may fulfill
his office and calling as willingly and faithfully[3] as the angels do in
heaven.[4]

[1] Matt. 16:24. [2] Lk. 22:42; Tit. 2:12. [3] 1 Cor. 7:24. [4] Ps. 103:20–21; *Rom. 12:2;
*Heb. 13:21.

LORD'S DAY 50

125. What is the fourth petition?

"Give us this day our daily bread;" that is, be pleased to provide for
all our bodily need,[1] so that we may thereby acknowledge that You
are the only fountain of all good,[2] and that without Your blessing
neither our care and labor, nor Your gifts, can profit us;[3] that we
may therefore withdraw our trust from all creatures and place it in
You alone.[4]

[1] Ps. 104:27–28; 145:15–16; Matt. 6:25–26. [2] Acts 14:17; 17:27–28. [3] 1 Cor. 15:58;
Deut. 8:3; Ps. 37:3–7, 16–17. [4] Ps. 55:22; 62:10; *Ps. 127:1–2; *Jer. 17:5, 7; *Ps. 146:2–3.

LORD'S DAY 51

126. What is the fifth petition?

"And forgive us our debts, as we forgive our debtors;" that is, be
pleased, for the sake of Christ's blood, not to impute to us miserable
sinners our manifold transgressions, nor the evil which always clings
to us;[1] as we also find this witness of Your grace in us, that it is our
full purpose heartily to forgive our neighbor.[2]

[1] Ps. 51:1–4; 143:2; 1 Jn. 2:1–2. [2] Matt. 6:14–15; Ps. 51:5–7; *Eph. 1:7.

LORD'S DAY 52

127. What is the sixth petition?

"And do not lead us into temptation, but deliver us from the evil
one;" that is, since we are so weak in ourselves that we cannot stand
a moment,[1] and besides, our deadly enemies, the devil,[2] the world,[3]
and our own flesh,[4] assail us without ceasing, be pleased to preserve
and strengthen us by the power of Your Holy Spirit, that we may

make firm stand against them and not be overcome in this spiritual warfare,[5] until finally complete victory is ours.[6]

[1] Jn. 15:5; Ps. 103:14–16. [2] 1 Pet. 5:8–9; Eph. 6:12–13. [3] Jn. 15:19. [4] Rom. 7:23; Gal. 5:17. [5] Matt. 26:41; Mk. 13:33. [6] 1 Thess. 3:13; 5:23–24; *2 Cor. 12:7.

128. How do you close this prayer?

"For Yours is the kingdom, and the power, and the glory, for ever;" that is, all this we ask of You, because as our King, having power over all things, You are willing and able to give us all good;[1] and that thereby not we, but Your holy name may be glorified for ever.[2]

[1] Rom. 10:11–12; 2 Pet. 2:9. [2] Jn. 14:13; Ps. 115:1.

129. What is the meaning of the word "Amen"?

"Amen" means: so shall it truly and surely be. For my prayer is much more certainly heard of God than I feel in my heart that I desire these things of Him.[1]

[1] 2 Cor. 1:20; 2 Tim. 2:13; *Ps. 145:18–19.

"Now to Him who is able to do exceedingly abundantly above
all that we ask or think, according to the power
that works in us, to Him be glory
in the church by Christ Jesus
to all generations,
forever and ever.
Amen."
—Ephesians 3:20–21

ন্ত

THE BELGIC
CONFESSION
OF FAITH

৪১

Introduction

ଔ

THIS DOCTRINAL STANDARD of the Reformed Church in the U.S. is called the Belgic Confession because it originated in the Southern Netherlands (Lowlands), now known as Belgium. Its chief author, Guido de Brès, born at Mons in 1523, was converted to the evangelical faith through the diligent reading of the Bible. Under Philip II of Spain, an ally of the Romish Church, believers in the Lowlands were sorely persecuted as revolutionaries. This Confession was written to prove that the Reformed believers were law-abiding citizens who professed only those doctrines which were in harmony with Holy Scripture.

The document was prepared in French by de Brès in 1561 and printed by 1566. Its composition is built to a great extent on the confession of the Reformed Churches in France, written chiefly by John Calvin and published two years earlier. The work of de Brès, however, is not a mere revision of that work, but an independent composition. It gives a more expanded treatment on the Trinity, the Incarnation, the Church, and the Sacraments. In his labors, de Brès was aided by Adrien de Savaria, Herman Modet, and G. Wingen. The work was revised by Francis Junius (1575–1602), a student of Calvin and pastor at Antwerp.

A copy was sent to the Spanish king in which it was bravely declared that these believers were ready to obey the government in all lawful things, although they would "offer their backs to stripes, their tongues to knives, their mouths to gags, and their whole bodies to fire, rather than deny the truth of God's Word."

Though the confession failed to stem the tide of persecution, it was instrumental in helping thousands understand the Reformed faith. Guido de Brès was eventually captured and he sealed his confession with martyr's blood in 1567. His work has endured as an expression of the faith of a people enduring suffering for Christ's sake, and will continue to serve as a means of instruction in the Reformed faith.

The Belgic Confession was adopted by the Reformed Church in the Netherlands at the Synod of Antwerp in 1566 and by the Reformed Church at Emden in 1571. After careful revision of the text, the Great Synod of Dort in 1618–19 adopted this confession as one of the doctrinal standards of the Reformed churches, to which all office-bearers (ministers, elders, deacons, professors of theology, and schoolmasters) of the churches were required to subscribe. Its excellence as one of the best statements of Reformed doctrine has been generally recognized by all Reformed churches.

The text used here is derived from the *Psalter Hymnal* of the Christian Reformed Church (1959). The Bible references are taken from the *New King James Version*.

THE BELGIC CONFESSION OF FAITH

ॐ

ARTICLE 1
THERE IS ONLY ONE GOD

We all believe with the heart and confess with the mouth that there is one only simple and spiritual Being, which we call God; and that He is eternal, incomprehensible, invisible, immutable, infinite, almighty, perfectly wise, just, good, and the overflowing fountain of all good.

ARTICLE 2
BY WHAT MEANS GOD IS MADE KNOWN UNTO US

We know Him by two means: First, by the creation, preservation, and government of the universe; which is before our eyes as a most elegant book, wherein all creatures, great and small, are as so many characters leading us to *see clearly His invisible attributes, even His eternal power and Godhead,* as the Apostle Paul says (Rom. 1:20). All which things are sufficient to convince men and leave them without excuse. Second, He makes Himself more clearly and fully known to us by His holy and divine Word, that is to say, as far as is necessary for us to know in this life, to His glory and our salvation.

ARTICLE 3
THE WRITTEN WORD OF GOD

We confess that this Word of God was not sent nor delivered by the will of man, but that *holy men of God spoke as they were moved by the Holy Spirit,* as the Apostle Peter says (2 Pet. 1:21); and that afterwards God, from a special care which He has for us and our salvation, commanded His servants, the prophets and apostles, to commit His revealed word to writing; and He Himself wrote with His own finger the two tables of the law. Therefore we call such writings holy and divine Scriptures.

ARTICLE 4
CANONICAL BOOKS OF THE HOLY SCRIPTURE

We believe that the Holy Scriptures are contained in two books, namely, the Old and the New Testament, which are canonical, against which nothing can be alleged. These are thus named in the Church of God.

The books of the Old Testament are the five books of Moses, to wit: Genesis, Exodus, Leviticus, Numbers, Deuteronomy; the book of Joshua, Judges, Ruth, the two books of Samuel, the two of the Kings, two books of the Chronicles, Ezra, Nehemiah, Esther; Job, the Psalms, the three books of Solomon, namely, the Proverbs, Ecclesiastes, and the Song of Songs; the four great prophets, Isaiah, Jeremiah, (Lamentations), Ezekiel, and Daniel; and the twelve lesser prophets, namely, Hosea, Joel, Amos, Obadiah, Jonah, Micah, Nahum, Habakkuk, Zephaniah, Haggai, Zechariah, and Malachi.

Those of the New Testament are the four evangelists, to wit: Matthew, Mark, Luke, and John; the Acts of the Apostles; the thirteen epistles of the Apostle Paul, namely, one to the Romans, two to the Corinthians, one to the Galatians, one to the Ephesians, one to the Philippians, one to the Colossians, two to the Thessalonians, two to Timothy, one to Titus, one to Philemon; Hebrews; the seven epistles of the other apostles, namely, one of James, two of Peter, three of John, one of Jude; and the Revelation of the Apostle John.

Article 5
Whence the Holy Scriptures Derive
Their Dignity and Authority

We receive all these books, and these only, as holy and canonical, for the regulation, foundation, and confirmation of our faith; believing without any doubt all things contained in them, not so much because the Church receives and approves them as such, but more especially because the Holy Spirit witnesses in our hearts that they are from God, and also because they carry the evidence thereof in themselves. For the very blind are able to perceive that the things foretold in them are being fulfilled.

Article 6
The Difference Between the Canonical
and Apocryphal Books

We distinguish those sacred books from the apocryphal, viz: the third and fourth books of Esdras, the books of Tobit, Judith, Wisdom, Jesus Sirach, Baruch, the Appendix to the book of Esther, the Song of the Three Children in the Furnace, the History of Susannah, of Bell and the Dragon, the Prayer of Manasseh, and the two books of the Maccabees. All of which the Church may read and take instruction from, so far as they agree with the canonical books; but they are far from having such power and efficacy that we may from their testimony confirm any point of faith or of the Christian religion; much less may they be used to detract from the authority of the other, that is, the sacred books.

ARTICLE 7
THE SUFFICIENCY OF THE HOLY SCRIPTURES
TO BE THE ONLY RULE OF FAITH

We believe that those Holy Scriptures fully contain the will of God, and that whatsoever man ought to believe unto salvation is sufficiently taught therein. For since the whole manner of worship which God requires of us is written in them at large, it is unlawful for any one, though an apostle, to teach otherwise than we are now taught in the Holy Scriptures: *but even if we, or an angel from heaven*, as the Apostle Paul says (Gal. 1:8). For since it is forbidden to add to or take away anything from the Word of God (Deut. 12:32), it does thereby evidently appear that the doctrine thereof is most perfect and complete in all respects.

Neither may we consider any writings of men, however holy these men may have been, of equal value with those divine Scriptures, nor ought we to consider custom, or the great multitude, or antiquity, or succession of times and persons, or councils, decrees or statutes, as of equal value with the truth of God, since the truth is above all; *for all men are of themselves liars, and lighter than vapor* (Ps. 62:9). Therefore we reject with all our hearts whatever does not agree with this infallible rule, as the apostles have taught us, saying, *Test the spirits, whether they are of God* (1 Jn. 4:1). Likewise: *If anyone comes to you and does not bring this doctrine, do not receive him into your house* (2 Jn. 1:10).

ARTICLE 8
GOD IS ONE IN ESSENCE,
YET DISTINGUISHED IN THREE PERSONS

According to this truth and this Word of God, we believe in one only God, who is the one single essence, in which are three Persons, really, truly, and eternally distinct according to their incommunicable properties; namely, the Father, and the Son, and the Holy Spirit. The Father is the cause, origin, and beginning of all things visible and invisible; the Son is the word, wisdom, and the image of the Father; the Holy Spirit is the eternal power and might, proceeding from the Father and the Son. Nevertheless, God is not by this distinction divided into three, since the Holy Scriptures teach us that the Father, and the Son, and the Holy Spirit have each His personality, distinguished by Their properties; but in such wise that these three Persons are but one only God.

Hence, then, it is evident that the Father is not the Son, nor the Son the Father, and likewise the Holy Spirit is neither the Father nor the Son. Nevertheless, these Persons thus distinguished are not divided, nor intermixed; for the Father has not assumed the flesh, nor has the Holy Spirit, but the Son only. The Father has never been without His Son, or without His Holy Spirit. For They are all three co-eternal and co-essential. There is neither first nor last; for They are all three one, in truth, in power, in goodness, and in mercy.

ARTICLE 9
THE PROOF OF THE FOREGOING ARTICLE OF
THE TRINITY OF PERSONS IN ONE GOD

All this we know as well from the testimonies of Holy Writ as from their operations, and chiefly by those we feel in ourselves. The testimonies of the Holy Scriptures that teach us to believe this Holy Trinity are written in many places of the Old Testament, which are not so necessary to enumerate as to choose them out with discretion and judgment.

In Genesis 1:26–27, God says: *Let Us make man in our image, according to Our likeness*, etc. *So God created man in His own image, male and female He created them.* And Genesis 3:22, *Behold, the man has become like one of Us.* From this saying, *Let Us make man in our image*, it appears that there are more persons than one in the Godhead; and when He says, God created, He signifies the unity. It is true, He does not say how many persons there are, but that which appears to us somewhat obscure in the Old Testament is very plain in the New. For when our Lord was baptized in Jordan, the voice of the Father was heard, saying, *This is My beloved Son* (Matt. 3:17); the Son was seen in the water, and the Holy Spirit appeared in the shape of a dove. This form is also instituted by Christ in the baptism of all believers: *Make disciples of all the nations, baptizing them in the name of the Father and of the Son and of the Holy Spirit* (Matt. 28:19). In the Gospel of Luke the angel Gabriel thus addressed Mary, the mother of our Lord: *The Holy Spirit will come upon you, and the power of the Highest will overshadow you; therefore also that Holy One who is to be born will be called the Son of God* (Lk. 1:35). Likewise: *The grace of the Lord Jesus Christ, and the love of God, and the communion of the Holy Spirit, be with you all* (2 Cor. 13:14). And: *There are three that bear witness in heaven, the Father, the Word, and the Holy Spirit; and these three are one* (1 Jn. 5:7).

In all these places we are fully taught that there are three Persons in one only divine essence. And although this doctrine far surpasses all human understanding, nevertheless we now believe it by means of the Word of God, but expect hereafter to enjoy the perfect knowledge and benefit thereof in heaven.

Moreover, we must observe the particular offices and operations of these three Persons towards us. The Father is called our Creator, by His power; the Son is our Savior and Redeemer, by His blood; the Holy Spirit is our Sanctifier, by His dwelling in our hearts.

This doctrine of the Holy Trinity has always been affirmed and maintained by the true Church since the time of the apostles to this very day against the Jews, Mohammedans, and some false Christians and heretics, as Marcion, Manes, Praxeas, Sabellius, Samosatenus, Arius, and such like, who have been justly condemned by the orthodox fathers. Therefore, in this point, we do willingly receive the three creeds, namely, that of the Apostles, of Nicea, and of Athanasius; likewise that which, conformable thereunto, is agreed upon by the ancient fathers.

ARTICLE 10
JESUS CHRIST IS TRUE AND ETERNAL GOD

We believe that Jesus Christ according to His divine nature is the only begotten Son of God, begotten from eternity, not made, nor created (for then He would be a creature), but co-essential and co-eternal with the Father, *the brightness of His glory and the express image of His person* (Heb. 1:3), equal unto Him in all things. He is the Son of God, not only from the time that He assumed our nature but from all eternity, as these testimonies, when compared together, teach us. Moses says that God created the world; and the Apostle John says that all things were made by that Word which he calls God. The apostle says that God made the world by His Son; likewise, that God created all things by Jesus Christ. Therefore it must needs follow that He who is called God, the Word, the Son, and Jesus Christ, did exist at that time when all things were created by Him. Therefore the prophet Micah says: *His goings forth have been from of old, from everlasting* (Mic. 5:2). And the apostle: *having neither beginning of days nor end of life* (Heb. 7:3). He therefore is that true, eternal, and almighty God whom we invoke, worship, and serve.

ARTICLE 11
THE HOLY SPIRIT IS TRUE AND ETERNAL GOD

We believe and confess also that the Holy Spirit from eternity proceeds from the Father and the Son; and therefore neither is made, created, nor begotten, but only proceeds from both; who in order is the third Person of the Holy Trinity; of one and the same essence, majesty, and glory with the Father and the Son; and therefore is the true and eternal God, as the Holy Scriptures teach us.

ARTICLE 12
THE CREATION OF ALL THINGS, ESPECIALLY THE ANGELS

We believe that the Father by the Word, that is, by His Son, has created of nothing the heaven, the earth, and all creatures, when it seemed good unto Him; giving unto every creature its being, shape, form, and several offices to serve its Creator; that He also still upholds and governs them by His eternal providence and infinite power for the service of mankind, to the end that man may serve his God.

He also created the angels good, to be His messengers and to serve His elect; some of whom are fallen from that excellency in which God created them into everlasting perdition, and the others have by the grace of God remained steadfast and continued in their first state. The devils and evil spirits are so depraved that they are enemies of God and every good thing; to the utmost of their power as murderers watching to ruin the Church and every member thereof, and by their wicked stratagems to destroy all; and are, therefore, by their own wickedness adjudged to eternal damnation, daily expecting their horrible torments.

Therefore we reject and abhor the error of the Sadducees, who deny the existence of spirits and angels; and also that of the Manichees, who assert that the devils have their origin of themselves, and that they are wicked of their own nature, without having been corrupted.

ARTICLE 13
THE PROVIDENCE OF GOD AND HIS GOVERNMENT OF ALL THINGS

We believe that the same good God, after He had created all things, did not forsake them or give them up to fortune or chance, but that He rules and governs them according to His holy will, so that nothing happens in this world without His appointment; nevertheless, God neither is the Author of nor can be charged with the sins which are committed.

For His power and goodness are so great and incomprehensible that He orders and executes His work in the most excellent and just manner, even then when devils and wicked men act unjustly. And as to what He does surpassing human understanding, we will not curiously inquire into farther than our capacity will admit of; but with the greatest humility and reverence adore the righteous judgments of God, which are hid from us, contenting ourselves that we are pupils of Christ, to learn only those things which He has revealed to us in His Word, without transgressing these limits.

This doctrine affords us unspeakable consolation, since we are taught thereby that nothing can befall us by chance, but by the direction of our most gracious and heavenly Father; who watches over us with a paternal care, keeping all creatures so under His power that not a hair of our head (for they are all numbered), nor a sparrow can fall to the ground without the will of our Father (Matt. 10:29–30), in whom we do entirely trust; being persuaded that He so restrains the devil and all our enemies that without His will and permission they cannot hurt us.

And therefore we reject that damnable error of the Epicureans, who say that God regards nothing but leaves all things to chance.

ARTICLE 14
THE CREATION AND FALL OF MAN,
AND HIS INCAPACITY TO PERFORM WHAT IS TRULY GOOD

We believe that God created man out of the dust of the earth, and made and formed him after His own image and likeness, good, righteous, and holy, capable in all things to will agreeably to the will of God. But *being in honor, he understood it not,* neither knew his excellency, but willfully subjected himself to sin and consequently to death and the curse, giving ear to the words of the devil. For the commandment of life, which he had received, he transgressed; and by sin separated himself from God, who was his true life; having corrupted his whole nature; whereby he made himself liable to corporal and spiritual death. And being thus become wicked, perverse, and corrupt in all his ways, he has lost all his excellent gifts which he had received from God, and retained only small remains thereof, which, however, are sufficient to leave man without excuse; for all the light which is in us is changed into darkness, as the Scriptures teach us, saying: *The light shines in the darkness, and the darkness did not comprehend it* (Jn. 1:5); where the Apostle John calls men darkness.

Therefore we reject all that is taught repugnant to this concerning the free will of man, since man is but a slave to sin, and *can receive nothing, unless it has been given to him from heaven* (Jn. 3:27). For who may presume to boast that he of himself can do any good, since Christ says: *No one can come to Me, unless the Father who sent Me draws him* (Jn. 6:44)? Who will glory in his own will, who understands that *the carnal mind is enmity against God* (Rom. 8:7)? Who can speak of his knowledge, since *the natural man does not receive the things of the Spirit of God* (1 Cor. 2:14)? In short, who dares suggest any thought, since he knows that *we are not sufficient of ourselves to think of anything as being from ourselves, but that our sufficiency is from God* (2 Cor. 3:5)? And therefore what the apostle says ought justly to be held sure and firm, that *God works in us both to will and to do for His good pleasure* (Phil. 2:13). For there is no understanding nor will conformable to the divine understanding and will but what Christ has wrought in man; which He teaches us, when He says: *Without Me you can do nothing* (Jn. 15:5).

ARTICLE 15
ORIGINAL SIN

We believe that through the disobedience of Adam original sin is extended to all mankind; which is a corruption of the whole nature and a hereditary disease, wherewith even infants in their mother's womb are infected, and which produces in man all sorts of sin, being in him as a root thereof, and therefore is so vile and abominable in the sight of God that it is sufficient to condemn all mankind. Nor is it altogether abolished or wholly eradicated even by regeneration; since sin always issues forth from this woeful source, as water from a fountain; notwithstanding it is not imputed to the children of God unto condemnation, but by His grace and mercy is forgiven them. Not that they should rest securely in sin, but that a sense of this corruption should make believers often to sigh, desiring to be delivered from this body of death.

Wherefore we reject the error of the Pelagians, who assert that sin proceeds only from imitation.

ARTICLE 16
ETERNAL ELECTION

We believe that, all the posterity of Adam being thus fallen into perdition and ruin by the sin of our first parents, God then did manifest Himself such as He is; that is to say, merciful and just: *merciful*, since He delivers and preserves from this perdition all whom He in His eternal and unchangeable counsel of mere goodness has elected in Christ Jesus our

Lord, without any respect to their works; *just*, in leaving others in the fall and perdition wherein they have involved themselves.

ARTICLE 17
THE RECOVERY OF FALLEN MAN

We believe that our most gracious God, in His admirable wisdom and goodness, seeing that man had thus thrown himself into physical and spiritual death and made himself wholly miserable, was pleased to seek and comfort him, when he trembling fled from His presence, promising him that He would give His Son (who would be *born of a woman* [Gal. 4:4]) to bruise the head of the serpent (Gen. 3:15) and to make him blessed.

ARTICLE 18
THE INCARNATION OF JESUS CHRIST

We confess, therefore, that God has fulfilled the promise which He made to the fathers by the mouth of His holy prophets, when He sent into the world, at the time appointed by Him, His own only-begotten and eternal Son, who *took the form of a servant* and *came in the likeness of men* (Phil. 2:7), really assuming the true human nature with all its infirmities, sin excepted; being conceived in the womb of the blessed virgin Mary by the power of the Holy Spirit without the means of man; and did not only assume human nature as to the body, but also a true human soul, that He might be a real man. For since the soul was lost as well as the body, it was necessary that He should take both upon Him, to save both.

Therefore we confess (in opposition to the heresy of the Anabaptists, who deny that Christ assumed human flesh of His mother) that Christ *partook of the flesh and blood of the children* (Heb. 2:14); that He is a *fruit of the body of David according to the flesh* (Acts 2:30); *born of the seed of David according to the flesh* (Rom. 1:3); *a fruit of the womb of Mary* (Lk. 1:42); *born of a woman* (Gal. 4:4); *a branch of David* (Jer. 33:15); *a Rod from the stem of Jesse* (Isa. 11:1); *sprung from the tribe of Judah* (Heb. 7:14); descended from the Jews according to the flesh; of the seed of Abraham, since *He took on Him the seed of Abraham* (Gal. 3:16), and *was made like His brethren in all things, sin excepted* (Heb. 2:17; 4:15); so that in truth He is our IMMANUEL, that is to say, *God with us* (Matt.1:23).

ARTICLE 19
THE UNION AND DISTINCTION OF THE
TWO NATURES IN THE PERSON OF CHRIST

We believe that by this conception the Person of the Son is inseparably united and connected with the human nature; so that there are not two Sons of God, nor two Persons, but two natures united in one single Person; yet each nature retains its own distinct properties. As, then, the divine nature has always remained uncreated, without beginning of days or end of life, filling heaven and earth, so also has the human nature not lost its properties but remained a creature, having beginning of days, being a finite nature, and retaining all the properties of a real body. And though He has by His resurrection given immortality to the same, nevertheless He has not changed the reality of His human nature; forasmuch as our salvation and resurrection also depend on the reality of His body.

But these two natures are so closely united in one Person that they were not separated even by His death. Therefore that which He, when dying, commended into the hands of His Father, was a real human spirit, departing from His body. But in the meantime the divine nature always remained united with the human, even when He lay in the grave; and the Godhead did not cease to be in Him, any more than it did when He was an infant, though it did not so clearly manifest itself for a while. Wherefore we confess that He is *very God* and *very man*: very God by His power to conquer death; and very man that He might die for us according to the infirmity of His flesh.

ARTICLE 20
GOD HAS MANIFESTED HIS JUSTICE AND MERCY IN CHRIST

We believe that God, who is perfectly merciful and just, sent His Son to assume that nature in which the disobedience was committed, to make satisfaction in the same, and to bear the punishment of sin by His most bitter passion and death. God therefore manifested His justice against His Son when He laid our iniquities upon Him, and poured forth His mercy and goodness on us, who were guilty and worthy of damnation, out of mere and perfect love, giving His Son unto death for us, and raising Him for our justification, that through Him we might obtain immortality and life eternal.

ARTICLE 21
THE SATISFACTION OF CHRIST, OUR ONLY HIGH PRIEST, FOR US

We believe that Jesus Christ is ordained with an oath to be an everlasting High Priest, after the order of Melchizedek; and that He has presented Himself in our behalf before the Father, to appease His wrath by His full satisfaction, by offering Himself on the tree of the cross, and pouring out His precious blood to purge away our sins, as the prophets had foretold. For it is written: *He was wounded for our transgressions, He was bruised for our iniquities; the chastisement for our peace was upon Him; and by His stripes we are healed. He was led as a lamb to the slaughter, and was numbered with the transgressors* (Isa. 53:5, 7, 12); and condemned by Pontius Pilate as a malefactor, though he had first declared Him innocent. Therefore, He restored that which He took not away (Ps. 69:4), and *suffered, the just for the unjust* (1 Pet. 3:18), as well in His body as in His soul, feeling the terrible punishment which our sins had merited; insomuch that *His sweat became like great drops of blood falling down to the ground* (Lk. 22:44). He called out: *My God, My God, why have You forsaken Me?* (Matt. 27:46) and has suffered all this for the remission of our sins.

Wherefore we justly say with the Apostle Paul that we know nothing *except Jesus Christ, and Him crucified* (1 Cor. 2:2); *we count all things loss for the excellence of the knowledge of Christ Jesus our Lord* (Phil. 3:8), in whose wounds we find all manner of consolation. Neither is it necessary to seek or invent any other means of being reconciled to God than this only sacrifice, once offered, by which *He has perfected forever those who are being sanctified* (Heb. 10:14). This is also the reason why He was called by the angel of God, JESUS, that is to say, SAVIOR, because He would save His people from their sins.

ARTICLE 22
OUR JUSTIFICATION THROUGH FAITH IN JESUS CHRIST

We believe that, to attain the true knowledge of this great mystery, the Holy Spirit kindles in our hearts an upright faith, which embraces Jesus Christ with all His merits, appropriates Him, and seeks nothing more besides Him. For it must needs follow, either that all things which are requisite to our salvation are not in Jesus Christ, or if all things are in Him, that then those who possess Jesus Christ through faith have complete salvation in Him. Therefore, for any to assert that Christ is not sufficient, but that something more is required besides Him, would be too gross a blasphemy; for hence it would follow that Christ was but half a Savior.

Therefore we justly say with Paul, that we *are justified by faith* alone, or *by faith apart from the deeds of the law* (Rom. 3:28). However, to speak more clearly, we do not mean that faith itself justifies us, for it is only an instrument with which we embrace Christ our righteousness. But Jesus Christ, imputing to us all His merits, and so many holy works which He has done for us and in our stead, is our righteousness. And faith is an instrument that keeps us in communion with Him in all His benefits, which, when they become ours, are more than sufficient to acquit us of our sins.

ARTICLE 23
WHEREIN OUR JUSTIFICATION BEFORE GOD CONSISTS

We believe that our salvation consists in the remission of our sins for Jesus Christ's sake, and that therein our righteousness before God is implied; as David and Paul teach us, declaring this to be the blessedness of man that *God imputes righteousness apart from works* (Rom 4:6; Ps. 32:1). And the same apostle says that we are *justified freely by His grace, through the redemption that is in Christ Jesus* (Rom. 3:24).

And therefore we always hold fast this foundation, ascribing all the glory to God, humbling ourselves before Him, and acknowledging ourselves to be such as we really are, without presuming to trust in any thing in ourselves, or in any merit of ours, relying and resting upon the obedience of Christ crucified alone, which becomes ours when we believe in Him. This is sufficient to cover all our iniquities, and to give us confidence in approaching to God; freeing the conscience of fear, terror, and dread, without following the example of our first father, Adam, who, trembling, attempted to cover himself with fig leaves. And, verily, if we should appear before God, relying on ourselves or on any other creature, though ever so little, we should, alas! be consumed. And therefore every one must pray with David: *O Lord, do not enter into judgment with Your servant, for in Your sight no one living is righteous* (Ps. 143:2).

ARTICLE 24
MAN'S SANCTIFICATION AND GOOD WORKS

We believe that this true faith, being wrought in man by the hearing of the Word of God and the operation of the Holy Spirit, sanctifies him and makes him a new man, causing him to live a new life, and freeing him from the bondage of sin. Therefore it is so far from being true that this justifying faith makes men remiss in a pious and holy life, that on the contrary without it they would never do anything out of love to God, but only out of self-love or fear of damnation. Therefore it is impossible that this holy faith can be unfruitful in man; for we do not speak of a vain faith, but of such a faith which is called in Scripture a *faith working through love* (Gal. 5:6), which excites man to the practice of those works which God has commanded in His Word.

These works, as they proceed from the good root of faith, are good and acceptable in the sight of God, forasmuch as they are all sanctified by His grace. Nevertheless they are of no account towards our justification, for it is by faith in Christ that we are justified, even before we do good works; otherwise they could not be good works, any more than the fruit of a tree can be good before the tree itself is good.

Therefore we do good works, but not to merit by them (for what can we merit?); nay, we are indebted to God for the good works we do, and not He to us, since it is He who *works in us both to will and to do for His good pleasure* (Phil. 2:13). Let us therefore attend to what is written: *When you have done all those things which you are commanded, say, "We are unprofitable servants. We have done what was our duty to do* (Lk. 17:10). In the meantime we do not deny that God rewards good works, but it is through His grace that He crowns His gifts.

Moreover, though we do good works, we do not found our salvation upon them; for we can do no work but what is polluted by our flesh, and also punishable; and although we could perform such works, still the remembrance of one sin is sufficient to make God reject them. Thus, then, we would always be in doubt, tossed to and fro without any certainty, and our poor consciences would be continually vexed if they relied not on the merits of the suffering and death of our Savior.

ARTICLE 25
THE ABOLISHING OF THE CEREMONIAL LAW

We believe that the ceremonies and symbols of the law ceased at the coming of Christ, and that all the shadows are accomplished; so that the use of them must be abolished among Christians; yet the truth and substance of them remain with us in Jesus Christ, in whom they have their completion. In the meantime we still use the testimonies taken out of the law and the prophets to confirm us in the doctrine of the gospel, and to regulate our life in all honorableness to the glory of God, according to His will.

ARTICLE 26
CHRIST'S INTERCESSION

We believe that we have no access unto God but alone through the only Mediator and Advocate, Jesus Christ the righteous; who therefore became man, having united in one Person the divine and human natures, that we men might have access to the divine Majesty, which access would otherwise be barred against us. But this Mediator, whom the Father has appointed between Him and us, ought in no wise to affright us by His majesty, or cause us to seek another according to our fancy. For there is no creature, either in heaven or on earth, who loves us more than Jesus Christ; *who, being in the form of God, made Himself of no reputation, taking the form of a bondservant, and coming in the likeness of men* for us (Phil. 2:6–7), and *in all things He had to be made like His brethren* (Heb. 2:17). If, then, we should seek for another mediator who would be favorably inclined towards us, whom could we find who loved us more than He who laid down His life for us, even while we were His enemies (Rom. 5:8, 10)? And if we seek for one who has power and majesty, who is there that has so much of both as He *who is seated at the right hand of the throne of the Majesty* (Heb. 8:1) and to whom has been given all authority in heaven and on earth (Matt. 28:18)? And who will sooner be heard than the own well-beloved Son of God?

Therefore it was only through distrust that this practice of dishonoring, instead of honoring, the saints was introduced, doing that which they never have done nor required, but have on the contrary steadfastly rejected according to their bounden duty, as appears by their writings. Neither must we plead here our unworthiness; for the meaning is not that we should offer our prayers to God on the ground of our own worthiness, but only on the ground of the excellency and worthiness of the Lord Jesus Christ, whose righteousness is become ours by faith.

Therefore the apostle, to remove this foolish fear, or rather distrust, from us, rightly says that Jesus Christ *in all things was made like His brethren, that He might be a merciful and faithful High Priest, to make propitiation for the sins of the people. For in that He himself has suffered, being tempted, He is able to aid those who are tempted* (Heb. 2:17–18). And further to encourage us to go to Him, He says: *Seeing then that we have a great High Priest who has passed through the heavens, Jesus the Son of God, let us hold fast our confession. For we do not have a High Priest who cannot sympathize with our weaknesses, but was in all points tempted as we are, yet without sin. Let us therefore come boldly to the throne of grace, that we may obtain mercy and find grace to help in time of need* (Heb. 4:14–15). The same apostle says: *Having boldness to enter the Holiest by the blood of Jesus, let us draw near with a true heart in full assurance of faith,* etc. (Heb. 10:19, 22). Likewise: *He . . . has an unchangeable priesthood; therefore He is also able to save to the uttermost those who come to God through Him, since He ever lives to make intercession for them* (Heb. 7:24–25).

What more can be required? Since Christ Himself says: *I am the way, the truth, and the life. No one comes to the Father except through Me* (Jn. 14:6). To what purpose should we, then, seek another advocate, since it has pleased God to give us His own Son as an Advocate? Let us not forsake Him to take another, or rather to seek after another, without ever being able to find him; for God well knew, when He gave Him to us, that we were sinners.

Therefore, according to the command of Christ, we call upon the heavenly Father through Jesus Christ our only Mediator, as we are taught in the Lord's Prayer; being assured that whatever we ask of the Father in His Name will be granted us.

Article 27
The Catholic Christian Church

We believe and profess one catholic or universal Church, which is a holy congregation of true Christian believers, all expecting their salvation in Jesus Christ, being washed by His blood, sanctified and sealed by the Holy Spirit.

This Church has been from the beginning of the world, and will be to the end thereof; which is evident from this that Christ is an eternal King, which without subjects He cannot be. And this holy Church is preserved or supported by God against the rage of the whole world; though it sometimes for a while appears very small, and in the eyes of men to be reduced to nothing; as during the perilous reign of Ahab the Lord reserved unto Him seven thousand men who had not bowed their knees to Baal.

Furthermore, this holy Church is not confined, bound, or limited to a certain place or to certain persons, but is spread and dispersed over the whole world; and yet is joined and united with heart and will, by the power of faith, in one and the same Spirit.

ARTICLE 28
EVERY ONE IS BOUND TO
JOIN HIMSELF TO THE TRUE CHURCH

We believe, since this holy congregation is an assembly of those who are saved, and outside of it there is no salvation, that no person of whatsoever state or condition he may be, ought to withdraw from it, content to be by himself; but that all men are in duty bound to join and unite themselves with it; maintaining the unity of the Church; submitting themselves to the doctrine and discipline thereof; bowing their necks under the yoke of Jesus Christ; and as mutual members of the same body, serving to the edification of the brethren, according to the talents God has given them.

And that this may be the more effectually observed, it is the duty of all believers, according to the Word of God, to separate themselves from all those who do not belong to the Church, and to join themselves to this congregation, wheresoever God has established it, even though the magistrates and edicts of princes were against it, yea, though they should suffer death or any other corporal punishment. Therefore all those who separate themselves from the same or do not join themselves to it act contrary to the ordinance of God.

ARTICLE 29
THE MARKS OF THE TRUE CHURCH,
AND WHEREIN IT DIFFERS FROM THE FALSE CHURCH

We believe that we ought diligently and circumspectly to discern from the Word of God which is the true Church, since all sects which are in the world assume to themselves the name of the Church. But we speak not here of hypocrites, who are mixed in the Church with the good, yet are not of the Church, though externally in it; but we say that the body and communion of the true Church must be distinguished from all sects that call themselves the Church.

The marks by which the true Church is known are these: If the pure doctrine of the gospel is preached therein; if it maintains the pure administration of the sacraments as instituted by Christ; if church discipline is exercised in chastening of sin; in short, if all things are managed according to the pure Word of God, all things contrary thereto rejected, and Jesus Christ acknowledged as the only Head of the Church. Hereby the true Church may certainly be known, from which no man has a right to separate himself.

With respect to those who are members of the Church, they may be known by the marks of Christians; namely, by faith, and when, having received Jesus Christ the only Savior, they avoid sin, follow after righteousness, love the true God and their neighbor, neither turn aside to the right or left, and crucify the flesh with the works thereof. But this is not to be understood as if there did not remain in them great infirmities; but they fight against them through the Spirit all the days of their life, continually taking their refuge in the blood, death, passion, and obedience of our Lord Jesus Christ, in whom they have remission of sins, through faith in Him.

As for the false Church, it ascribes more power and authority to itself and its ordinances than to the Word of God, and will not submit itself to the yoke of Christ. Neither does it administer the sacraments as appointed by Christ in His Word, but adds to and takes from them, as it thinks proper; it relies more upon men than upon Christ; and persecutes those who live holily according to the Word of God and rebuke it for its errors, covetousness, and idolatry.

These two Churches are easily known and distinguished from each other.

ARTICLE 30
THE GOVERNMENT OF THE CHURCH AND ITS OFFICES

We believe that this true Church must be governed by that spiritual polity which our Lord has taught us in His Word; namely, that there must be ministers or pastors to preach the Word of God and to administer the sacraments; also elders and deacons, who, together with the pastors, form the council of the Church; that by these means the true religion may be preserved, and the true doctrine everywhere propagated, likewise transgressors chastened and restrained by spiritual means; also that the poor and distressed may be relieved and comforted, according to their necessities. By these means everything will be carried on in the Church with good order and decency, when faithful men are chosen, according to the rule prescribed by the Apostle Paul in his Epistle to Timothy.

ARTICLE 31
THE MINISTERS, ELDERS, AND DEACONS

We believe that the ministers of God's Word, the elders, and the deacons ought to be chosen to their respective offices by a lawful election by the Church, with calling upon the name of the Lord, and in that order which the Word of God teaches. Therefore everyone must take heed not to intrude himself by improper means, but is bound to wait till it shall please God to call him; that he may have testimony of his calling, and be certain and assured that it is of the Lord.

As for the ministers of God's Word, they have equally the same power and authority wheresoever they are, as they are all ministers of Christ, the only universal Bishop and the only Head of the Church.

Moreover, in order that this holy ordinance of God may not be violated or slighted, we say that every one ought to esteem the ministers of God's Word and the elders of the Church very highly for their work's sake, and be at peace with them without murmuring, strife, or contention, as much as possible.

ARTICLE 32
THE ORDER AND DISCIPLINE OF THE CHURCH

In the meantime we believe, though it is useful and beneficial that those who are rulers of the Church institute and establish certain ordinances among themselves for maintaining the body of the Church, yet that they ought studiously to take care that they do not depart from those things which Christ, our only Master, has instituted. And therefore we reject all human inventions, and all laws which man would introduce into the worship of God, thereby to bind and compel the conscience in any manner whatever. Therefore we admit only of that which tends to nourish and preserve concord and unity, and to keep all men in obedience to God. For this purpose, excommunication or church discipline is requisite, with all that pertains to it, according to the Word of God.

ARTICLE 33
THE SACRAMENTS

We believe that our gracious God, taking account of our weakness and infirmities, has ordained the sacraments for us, thereby to seal unto us His promises, and to be pledges of the good will and grace of God towards us, and also to nourish and strengthen our faith; which He has joined to the Word of the gospel, the better to present to our senses both that which He declares to us by His Word and that which He works inwardly in our hearts, thereby confirming in us the salvation which He imparts to us. For they are visible signs and seals of an inward and invisible thing, by means whereof God works in us by the power of the Holy Spirit. Therefore the signs are not empty or meaningless, so as to deceive us. For

Jesus Christ is the true object presented by them, without whom they would be of no moment.

Moreover, we are satisfied with the number of sacraments which Christ our Lord has instituted, which are two only, namely, the sacrament of baptism and the holy supper of our Lord Jesus Christ.

ARTICLE 34
HOLY BAPTISM

We believe and confess that Jesus Christ, who is the end of the law, has made an end, by the shedding of His blood, of all other sheddings of blood which men could or would make as a propitiation or satisfaction for sin; and that He, having abolished circumcision, which was done with blood, has instituted the sacrament of baptism instead thereof; by which we are received into the Church of God, and separated from all other people and strange religions, that we may wholly belong to Him whose mark and ensign we bear; and which serves as a testimony to us that He will forever be our gracious God and Father.

Therefore He has commanded all those who are His to be baptized with pure water, *in the name of the Father and of the Son and of the Holy Spirit* (Matt. 28:19), thereby signifying to us, that as water washes away the filth of the body when poured upon it, and is seen on the body of the baptized when sprinkled upon him, so does the blood of Christ by the power of the Holy Spirit internally sprinkle the soul, cleanse it from its sins, and regenerate us from children of wrath unto children of God. Not that this is effected by the external water, but by the sprinkling of the precious blood of the Son of God; who is our Red Sea, through which we must pass to escape the tyranny of Pharaoh, that is, the devil, and to enter into the spiritual land of Canaan.

The ministers, therefore, on their part administer the sacrament and that which is visible, but our Lord gives that which is signified by the sacrament, namely, the gifts and invisible grace; washing, cleansing, and purging our souls of all filth and unrighteousness; renewing our hearts and filling them with all comfort; giving unto us a true assurance of His fatherly goodness; putting on us the new man, and putting off the old man with all his deeds.

We believe, therefore, that every man who is earnestly studious of obtaining life eternal ought to be baptized but once with this only baptism, without ever repeating the same, since we cannot be born twice. Neither does this baptism avail us only at the time when the water is poured upon us and received by us, but also through the whole course of our life.

Therefore we detest the error of the Anabaptists, who are not content with the one only baptism they have once received, and moreover condemn the baptism of the infants of believers, who we believe ought to be baptized and sealed with the sign of the covenant, as the children in Israel formerly were circumcised upon the same promises which are made unto our children. And indeed Christ shed His blood no less for the washing of the children of believers than for adult persons; and therefore they ought to receive the sign and sacrament of that which Christ has done for them; as the Lord commanded in the law that they should be made partakers of the sacrament of Christ's suffering and death shortly after they were born, by offering for them a lamb, which was a sacrament of Jesus Christ. Moreover, what circumcision was to the Jews, baptism is to our children. And for this reason the Apostle Paul calls baptism *the circumcision of Christ* (Col. 2:11).

ARTICLE 35
THE HOLY SUPPER OF OUR LORD JESUS CHRIST

We believe and confess that our Savior Jesus Christ did ordain and institute the sacrament of the holy supper to nourish and support those whom He has already regenerated and incorporated into His family, which is His Church.

Now those who are regenerated have in them a twofold life, the one corporal and temporal, which they have from the first birth and is common to all men; the other, spiritual and heavenly, which is given them in their second birth, which is effected by the Word of the gospel, in the communion of the body of Christ; and this life is not common, but is peculiar to God's elect. In like manner God has given us, for the support of the bodily and earthly life, earthly and common bread, which is subservient thereto and is common to all men, even as life itself. But for the support of the spiritual and heavenly life which believers have He has sent a living bread, which descended from heaven, namely, Jesus Christ, who nourishes and strengthens the spiritual life of believers when they eat Him, that is to say, when they appropriate and receive Him by faith in the spirit.

In order that He might represent unto us this spiritual and heavenly bread, Christ has instituted an earthly and visible bread as a sacrament of His body, and wine as a sacrament of His blood, to testify by them unto us that, as certainly as we receive and hold this sacrament in our hands and eat and drink the same with our mouths, by which our life is afterwards nourished, we also do as certainly receive by faith (which is the hand and mouth of our soul) the true body and blood of Christ our only Savior in our souls, for the support of our spiritual life.

Now, as it is certain and beyond all doubt that Jesus Christ has not enjoined to us the use of His sacraments in vain, so He works in us all that He represents to us by these holy signs, though the manner surpasses our understanding and cannot be comprehended by us, as the operations of the Holy Spirit are hidden and incomprehensible. In the meantime we err not when we say that what is eaten and drunk by us is the proper and natural body and the proper blood of Christ. But the manner of our partaking of the same is not by the mouth, but by the spirit through faith. Thus, then, though Christ always sits at the right hand of His Father in the heavens, yet does He not therefore cease to make us partakers of Himself by faith. This feast is a spiritual table, at which Christ communicates Himself with all His benefits to us, and gives us there to enjoy both Himself and the merits of His sufferings and death: nourishing, strengthening, and comforting our poor comfortless souls by the eating of His flesh, quickening and refreshing them by the drinking of His blood.

Further, though the sacraments are connected with the thing signified nevertheless both are not received by all men. The ungodly indeed receives the sacrament to his condemnation, but he does not receive the truth of the sacrament, even as Judas and Simon the sorcerer both indeed received the sacrament but not Christ who was signified by it, of whom believers only are made partakers.

Lastly, we receive this holy sacrament in the assembly of the people of God, with humility and reverence, keeping up among us a holy remembrance of the death of Christ our Savior, with thanksgiving, making there confession of our faith and of the Christian religion. Therefore no one ought to come to this table without having previously rightly examined himself, lest by eating of this bread and drinking of this cup he eat and drink judgment to himself. In a word, we are moved by the use of this holy sacrament to a fervent love towards God and our neighbor.

Therefore we reject all mixtures and damnable inventions which men have added unto and blended with the sacraments, as profanations of them; and affirm that we ought to rest satisfied with the ordinance which Christ and His apostles have taught us, and that we must speak of them in the same manner as they have spoken.

ARTICLE 36
THE MAGISTRACY (CIVIL GOVERNMENT)

We believe that our gracious God, because of the depravity of mankind, has appointed kings, princes, and magistrates; willing that the world should be governed by certain laws and policies; to the end that the dissoluteness of men might be restrained, and all things carried on among them with good order and decency. For this purpose He has invested the magistracy with the sword for the punishment of him who practices evil and for the protection of those that do good (Rom. 13:4).

Their office is not only to have regard unto and watch for the welfare of the civil state, but also to protect the sacred ministry, that the kingdom of Christ may thus be promoted. They must therefore countenance the preaching of the Word of the gospel everywhere, that God may be honored and worshiped by every one, as He commands in His Word.

Moreover, it is the bounden duty of everyone, of whatever state, quality, or condition he may be, to subject himself to the magistrates; to pay tribute, to show due honor and respect to them, and to obey them in all things which are not repugnant to the Word of God; to supplicate for them in our prayers that God may rule and guide them in all their ways, and *that we may lead a quiet and peaceable life in all godliness and reverence* (1 Tim. 2:1–2).

Wherefore we detest the Anabaptists and other seditious people, and in general all those who reject the higher powers and magistrates and would subvert justice, introduce community of goods, and confound that decency and good order which God has established among men.

ARTICLE 37
THE LAST JUDGMENT

Finally, we believe, according to the Word of God, when the time appointed by the Lord (which is unknown to all creatures) is come and the number of the elect complete, that our Lord Jesus Christ will come from heaven, corporally and visibly, as He ascended, with great glory and majesty to declare Himself Judge of the living and the dead, burning this old world with fire and flame to cleanse it.

Then all men will personally appear before this great Judge, both men and women and children, that have been from the beginning of the world to the end thereof, being summoned by *the voice of an archangel, and with the trumpet of God* (1 Thess. 4:16). For all the dead shall be raised out of the earth, and their souls joined and united with their proper bodies in which they formerly lived. As for those who shall then be living, they shall not die as the others, but be changed in the twinkling of an eye, and from corruptible become incorruptible. Then books shall be opened, and the dead judged (Rev. 20:12) according to what they shall have done in this world, whether it be good or evil. Nay, *for every idle word men may speak, they will give account* (Matt. 12:36), which the world only counts amusement and jest; and then the secrets and hypocrisy of men shall be disclosed and laid open before all.

And therefore the consideration of this judgment is justly terrible and dreadful to the wicked and ungodly, but most desirable and comfortable to the righteous and elect; because then their full deliverance shall be perfected, and there they shall receive the fruits of their labor and trouble which they have borne. Their innocence shall be known to all, and they shall see the terrible vengeance which God shall execute on the wicked, who most cruelly persecuted, oppressed, and tormented them in this world, and who shall be convicted by the testimony of their own consciences, and shall become immortal, but only to be tormented in *the everlasting fire prepared for the devil and his angels* (Matt. 25:41).

But on the contrary, the faithful and elect shall be crowned with glory and honor; and the Son of God will confess their names before God His Father and His elect angels; all tears shall be wiped from their eyes; and their cause which is now condemned by many judges and magistrates as heretical and impious will then be known to be the cause of the Son of God. And for a gracious reward, the Lord will cause them to possess such a glory as never entered into the heart of man to conceive.

Therefore we expect that great day with a most ardent desire, to the end that we may fully enjoy the promises of God in Christ Jesus our Lord. AMEN.

Even so, come, Lord Jesus! (Rev. 22:20).

ca

THE CANONS
OF DORT

so

Introduction

ೲ

THE DECISION of the Synod of Dort on the "Five Main Points of Doctrine in Dispute" is popularly known as the Canons of Dort. This Great Synod met in the city of Dordrecht in the Netherlands during the years 1618–19 to settle a serious controversy in the Dutch churches initiated by the rise of Arminianism. Jacob Arminius, a theological professor at Leiden University, questioned the teaching of the Reformed churches on a number of important points and advocated a revision of the Belgic Confession and the Heidelberg Catechism. After Arminius's death, his followers presented their views on five of these points in the Remonstrance of 1610. The Arminians taught election based on foreseen faith, universal atonement, partial depravity, resistible grace, and the possibility of a lapse from grace.

Convened by the States-General of the Netherlands on November 13, 1618, as a national synod of the Reformed churches of the Netherlands, it became an international council as well, with twenty-seven representatives of foreign churches being invited to participate. With delegates from Germany (the Palatinate, Hesse, Bremen), Switzerland, and England, the Synod represented a consensus of all the Reformed Churches, bringing together many of the great Reformed theologians of the day. The services were public and crowded by spectators. Johannes Bogerman, pastor at Leuuwarden, presided. There were 154 sessions, the last of which was held May 9, 1619. When the Canons were completed, both the foreign and Dutch delegates affirmed them by their signatures, and a service of thanksgiving to God followed.

In the Canons the Synod set forth the Reformed doctrine on unconditional election, particular redemption, total depravity, irresistible grace, and the perseverance of the saints. The original preface called them a "judgment, in which both the true view, agreeing with God's Word concerning the aforesaid five points of doctrine is explained, and the false view, disagreeing with God's Word, is rejected." Because the Canons are an answer to the specific Five Points of the Remonstrance, they do not treat the whole of theology, but focus on the central doctrines of salvation which comprise the gospel. Although in form there are only four Heads of Doctrine, we speak properly of five points, because points three and four were combined into one Head.

Each of the Canons consists of a positive and a negative part, the former being an exposition of the Reformed doctrine on the subject, and the latter a refutation of the corresponding Arminian errors.

THE CANONS
OF DORT

ෆ

The First Head of Doctrine
DIVINE ELECTION AND REPROBATION

ARTICLE 1

As all men have sinned in Adam, lie under the curse, and are deserving of eternal death, God would have done no injustice by leaving them all to perish and delivering them over to condemnation on account of sin, according to the words of the apostle: *That every mouth may be stopped, and all the world may become guilty before God* (Rom. 3:19). *For all have sinned and fall short of the glory of God* (Rom. 3:23); and, *For the wages of sin is death* (Rom. 6:23).

ARTICLE 2

But in this the love of God was manifested, that He *sent His only begotten Son into the world, that whoever believes in Him should not perish but have everlasting life* (1 Jn. 4:9; Jn. 3:16).

ARTICLE 3

And that men may be brought to believe, God mercifully sends the messengers of these most joyful tidings to whom He will and at what time He pleases; by whose ministry men are called to repentance and faith in Christ crucified. *How then shall they call on Him in whom they have not believed? And how shall they believe in Him of whom they have not heard? And how shall they hear without a preacher? And how shall they preach unless they are sent?* (Rom. 10:14–15).

ARTICLE 4

The wrath of God abides upon those who believe not this gospel. But such as receive it and embrace Jesus the Savior by a true and living faith are by Him delivered from the wrath of God and from destruction, and have the gift of eternal life conferred upon them.

ARTICLE 5

The cause or guilt of this unbelief as well as of all other sins is no wise in God, but in man himself; whereas faith in Jesus Christ and salvation through Him is the free gift of God, as it is written: *For by grace you have been saved through faith; and that not of yourselves, it is the gift of God* (Eph. 2:8). Likewise, *To you it has been granted on behalf of Christ, not only to believe in Him*, etc. (Phil. 1:29).

ARTICLE 6

That some receive the gift of faith from God, and others do not receive it, proceeds from God's eternal decree. For *known to God from eternity are all His works* (Acts 15:18). *Who works all things according to the counsel of His will* (Eph. 1:11). According to which decree He graciously softens the hearts of the elect, however obstinate, and inclines them to believe; while He leaves the non-elect in His just judgment to their own wickedness and obduracy. And herein is especially displayed the profound, the merciful, and at the same time the righteous discrimination between men equally involved in ruin; or that decree of election and reprobation, revealed in the Word of God, which, though men of perverse, impure, and unstable minds wrest it to their own destruction, yet to holy and pious souls affords unspeakable consolation.

ARTICLE 7

Election is the unchangeable purpose of God, whereby, before the foundation of the world, He has out of mere grace, according to the sovereign good pleasure of His own will, chosen from the whole human race, which had fallen through their own fault from their primitive state of rectitude into sin and destruction, a certain number of persons to redemption in Christ, whom He from eternity appointed the Mediator and Head of the elect and the foundation of salvation. This elect number, though by nature neither better nor more deserving than others, but with them involved in one common misery, God has decreed to give to Christ to be saved by Him, and effectually to call and draw them to His communion by His Word and Spirit; to bestow upon them true faith, justification, and sanctification; and having powerfully preserved them in the fellowship of His Son, finally to glorify them for the demonstration of His mercy, and for the praise of the riches of His glorious grace; as it is written: *Just as He chose us in Him before the foundation of the world, that we should be holy and without blame before Him in love, having predestined us to adoption as sons by Jesus Christ to Himself, according to the good pleasure of His will, to the praise of the glory of His grace, by which He has made us accepted in the Beloved* (Eph. 1:4–6). And elsewhere, *Whom He predestined, these He also called; whom He called, these He also justified; and whom He justified, these He also glorified* (Rom. 8:30).

ARTICLE 8

There are not various decrees of election, but one and the same decree respecting all those who shall be saved, both under the Old and the New Testament; since the Scripture declares the good pleasure, purpose, and counsel of the divine will to be one, according to which He has chosen us from eternity, both to grace and to glory, to salvation and to the way of salvation, which He has ordained that we should walk therein (Eph. 1:4–5; 2:10).

ARTICLE 9

This election was not founded upon foreseen faith and the obedience of faith, holiness, or any other good quality or disposition in man, as the prerequisite, cause, or condition on which it depended; but men are chosen to faith and to the obedience of faith, holiness, etc. Therefore election is the fountain of every saving good, from which proceed faith, holiness, and the other gifts of salvation, and finally eternal life itself, as its fruits and effects, according to the testimony of the apostle: *He chose us in Him* (not because we were, but) *that we should be holy and without blame before Him in love* (Eph. 1:4).

ARTICLE 10

The good pleasure of God is the sole cause of this gracious election; which does not consist herein that out of all possible qualities and actions of men God has chosen some as a condition of salvation, but that He was pleased out of the common mass of sinners to adopt some certain persons as a peculiar people to Himself, as it is written: *For the children not yet being born, nor having done any good or evil,* etc., *it was said to her* (namely, to Rebekah), *"The older shall serve the younger." As it is written, "Jacob I have loved, but Esau I have hated"* (Rom. 9:11–13). *And as many as had been appointed to eternal life believed* (Acts 13:48).

ARTICLE 11

And as God Himself is most wise, unchangeable, omniscient, and omnipotent, so the election made by Him can neither be interrupted nor changed, recalled, or annulled; neither can the elect be cast away, nor their number diminished.

ARTICLE 12

The elect in due time, though in various degrees and in different measures, attain the assurance of this their eternal and unchangeable election, not by inquisitively prying into the secret and deep things of God, but by observing in themselves with a spiritual joy and holy pleasure the infallible fruits of election pointed out in the Word of God—such as, a true faith in Christ, filial fear, a godly sorrow for sin, a hungering and thirsting after righteousness, etc.

ARTICLE 13

The sense and certainty of this election afford to the children of God additional matter for daily humiliation before Him, for adoring the depth of His mercies, for cleansing themselves, and rendering grateful returns of ardent love to Him who first manifested so great love towards them. The consideration of this doctrine of election is so far from encouraging remissness in the observance of the divine commands or from sinking men in carnal security, that these, in the just judgment of God, are the usual effects of rash presumption or of idle and wanton trifling with the grace of election, in those who refuse to walk in the ways of the elect.

ARTICLE 14

As the doctrine of divine election by the most wise counsel of God was declared by the prophets, by Christ Himself, and by the apostles, and is clearly revealed in the Scriptures both of the Old and the New Testament, so it is still to be published in due time and place in the Church of God, for which it was peculiarly designed, provided it be done with reverence, in the spirit of discretion and piety, for the glory of God's most holy Name, and for enlivening and comforting His people, without vainly attempting to investigate the sacred ways of the Most High (Acts 20:27; Rom. 11:33, 34; 12:3; Heb. 6:17–18).

ARTICLE 15

What peculiarly tends to illustrate and recommend to us the eternal and unmerited grace of election is the express testimony of sacred Scripture that not all, but some only, are elected, while others are passed by in the eternal decree; whom God, out of His sovereign, most just, irreprehensible, and unchangeable good pleasure, has decreed to leave in the common misery into which they have willfully plunged themselves, and not to bestow upon them saving faith and the grace of conversion; but, permitting them in His just judgment to follow their own ways, at last, for the declaration of His justice, to condemn and punish them forever, not only on account of their unbelief, but also for all their other sins. And this is the decree of reprobation, which by no means makes God the Author of sin (the very thought of which is blasphemy), but declares Him to be an awful, irreprehensible, and righteous Judge and Avenger thereof.

ARTICLE 16

Those in whom a living faith in Christ, an assured confidence of soul, peace of conscience, an earnest endeavor after filial obedience, a glorying in God through Christ, is not as yet strongly felt, and who nevertheless make use of the means which God has appointed for working these graces in us, ought not to be alarmed at the mention of reprobation, nor to rank themselves among the reprobate, but diligently to persevere in the use of means, and with ardent desires devoutly and humbly to wait for a season of richer grace. Much less cause to be terrified by the doctrine of reprobation have they who, though they seriously desire to be turned to God, to please Him only, and to be delivered from the body of death, cannot yet reach that measure of holiness and faith to which they aspire; since a merciful God has promised that He will not quench the smoking flax, nor break the bruised reed. But this doctrine is justly terrible to those who, regardless of God and of the Savior Jesus Christ, have wholly given themselves up to the cares of the world and the pleasures of the flesh, so long as they are not seriously converted to God.

ARTICLE 17

Since we are to judge of the will of God from His Word, which testifies that the children of believers are holy, not by nature, but in virtue of the covenant of grace, in which they together with the parents are comprehended, godly parents ought not to doubt the election and salvation of their children whom it pleases God to call out of this life in their infancy (Gen. 17:7; Acts 2:39; 1 Cor. 7:14).

ARTICLE 18

To those who murmur at the free grace of election and the just severity of reprobation we answer with the apostle: *But indeed, O man, who are you to reply against God?* (Rom. 9:20), and quote the language of our Savior: *Is it not lawful for me to do what I wish with my own things?* (Matt. 20:15). And therefore, with holy adoration of these mysteries, we exclaim in the words of the apostle: *O the depth of the riches both of the wisdom and knowledge of God! How unsearchable are His judgments and His ways past finding out! For who has known the mind of the Lord? Or who has become His counselor? Or who has first given to Him and it shall be repaid to Him? For of Him and through Him and to Him are all things, to whom be glory forever. Amen.* (Rom. 11:33–36).

Rejection of Errors

The true doctrine concerning election and reprobation having been explained, the Synod rejects the errors of those:

PARAGRAPH 1

Error

Who teach: That the will of God to save those who would believe and would persevere in faith and in the obedience of faith is the whole and entire decree of election unto salvation, and that nothing else concerning this decree has been revealed in God's Word.

Refutation

For these deceive the simple and plainly contradict the Scriptures, which declare that God will not only save those who will believe, but that He has also from eternity chosen certain particular persons to whom, above others, He will grant, in time, both faith in Christ and perseverance, as it is written, *I have manifested Your name to the men whom You have given Me out of the world* (Jn. 17:6). *And as many as had been appointed to eternal life believed* (Acts 13:48); and, *Just as He chose us in Him before the foundation of the world, that we should be holy and without blame before Him in love* (Eph. 1:4).

PARAGRAPH 2

Error

Who teach: That there are various kinds of election of God unto eternal life: the one general and indefinite, the other particular and definite; and that the latter in turn is either incomplete, revocable, non-decisive, and conditional, or complete, irrevocable, decisive, and absolute. Likewise: That there is one election unto faith and another unto salvation, so that election can be unto justifying faith, without being a decisive election unto salvation.

Refutation

For this is a fancy of men's minds, invented regardless of the Scriptures, whereby the doctrine of election is corrupted, and this golden chain of our salvation is broken: *Moreover whom He predestined, these He also called; whom He called, these He also justified; and whom He justified, these He also glorified* (Rom. 8:30).

Paragraph 3

Error

Who teach: That the good pleasure and purpose of God, of which Scripture makes mention in the doctrine of election, does not consist in this, that God chose certain persons rather than others, but in this, that He chose out of all possible conditions (among which are also the works of the law), or out of the whole order of things, the act of faith which from its very nature is undeserving, as well as its incomplete obedience, as a condition of salvation, and that He would graciously consider this in itself as a complete obedience and count it worthy of the reward of eternal life.

Refutation

For by this injurious error the pleasure of God and the merits of Christ are made of none effect, and men are drawn away by useless questions from the truth of gracious justification and from the simplicity of Scripture, and this declaration of the apostle is charged as untrue: *Who has saved us and called us with a holy calling, not according to our works, but according to His own purpose and grace which was given to us in Christ Jesus before time began* (2 Tim. 1:9).

Paragraph 4

Error

Who teach: That in the election unto faith this condition is beforehand demanded that man should use his innate understanding of God aright, be pious, humble, meek, and fit for eternal life, as if on these things election were in any way dependent.

Refutation

For this savors of the teaching of Pelagius, and is opposed to the doctrine of the apostle when he writes, *Among whom also we all once conducted ourselves in the lusts of our flesh, fulfilling the desires of the flesh and of the mind, and were by nature children of wrath, just as the others. But God, who is rich in mercy, because of His great love with which He loved us, even when we were dead in trespasses, made us alive together with Christ (by grace you have been saved), and raised us up together, and made us sit together in the heavenly places in Christ Jesus, that in the ages to come He might show the exceeding riches of His grace in His kindness toward us in Christ Jesus. For by grace you have been saved through faith; and that not of yourselves; it is the gift of God, not of works, lest anyone should boast* (Eph. 2:3–9).

PARAGRAPH 5

Error

Who teach: That the incomplete and non-decisive election of particular persons to salvation occurred because of a foreseen faith, conversion, holiness, godliness, which either began or continued for some time; but that the complete and decisive election occurred because of foreseen perseverance unto the end in faith, conversion, holiness, and godliness; and that this is the gracious and evangelical worthiness, for the sake of which he who is chosen is more worthy than he who is not chosen; and that therefore faith, the obedience of faith, holiness, godliness, and perseverance are not fruits of the unchangeable election unto glory, but are conditions which, being required beforehand, were foreseen as being met by those who will be fully elected, and are causes without which the unchangeable election to glory does not occur.

Refutation

This is repugnant to the entire Scripture, which constantly inculcates this and similar declarations: *Election is not of works, but of Him who calls* (Rom. 9:11). *And as many as had been appointed to eternal life believed* (Acts 13:48). *He chose us in Him before the foundation of the world, that we should be holy* (Eph. 1:4). *You did not choose Me, but I chose you* (Jn. 15:16). *And if by grace, then it is no longer of works* (Rom. 11:6). *In this is love, not that we loved God, but that He loved us, and sent His Son* (1 Jn. 4:10).

PARAGRAPH 6

Error

Who teach: That not every election unto salvation is unchangeable, but that some of the elect, any decree of God notwithstanding, can yet perish and do indeed perish.

Refutation

By this gross error they make God to be changeable, and destroy the comfort which the godly obtain out of the firmness of their election, and contradict the Holy Scripture, which teaches that the elect can not be led astray (Matt. 24:24), that Christ does not lose those whom the Father gave Him (Jn. 6:39), and that God also glorified those whom He predestined, called, and justified (Rom. 8:30).

PARAGRAPH 7

Error

Who teach: That there is in this life no fruit and no consciousness of the unchangeable election to glory, nor any certainty, except that which depends on a changeable and uncertain condition.

Refutation

For not only is it absurd to speak of an uncertain certainty, but also contrary to the experience of the saints, who by virtue of the consciousness of their election rejoice with the apostle and praise this favor of God (Eph. 1); who according to Christ's admonition rejoice with His disciples that their *names are written in heaven* (Lk. 10:20); who also place the consciousness of their election over against the fiery darts of the devil, asking, *Who shall bring a charge against God's elect?* (Rom. 8:33).

PARAGRAPH 8

Error

Who teach: That God, simply by virtue of His righteous will, did not decide either to leave anyone in the fall of Adam and in the common state of sin and condemnation, or to pass anyone by in the communication of grace which is necessary for faith and conversion.

Refutation

For this is firmly decreed: *He has mercy on whom He wills, and whom He wills He hardens* (Rom. 9:18); and also this: *It has been given to you to know the mysteries of the kingdom of heaven, but to them it has not been given* (Matt. 13:11). Likewise, *I thank You, Father, Lord of heaven and earth, because You have hidden these things from the wise and prudent and have revealed them to babes. Even so, Father, for so it seemed good in Your sight* (Matt. 11:25–26).

PARAGRAPH 9

Error

Who teach: That the reason why God sends the gospel to one people rather than to another is not merely and solely the good pleasure of God, but rather the fact that one people is better and worthier than another to which the gospel is not communicated.

Refutation

For this Moses denies, addressing the people of Israel as follows: *Indeeed heaven and the highest heavens belong to the Lord your God, also the earth with all that is in it. The Lord delighted only in your fathers, to love them; and He chose their descendants after them, you above all peoples, as it is this day* (Deut. 10:14–15); and Christ said, *Woe to you, Chorazin! Woe to you, Bethsaida! For if the mighty works which were done in you had been done in Tyre and Sidon, they would have repented long ago in sackcloth and ashes* (Matt. 11:21).

The Second Head of Doctrine
THE DEATH OF CHRIST,
AND THE REDEMPTION OF MEN THEREBY

ARTICLE 1

God is not only supremely merciful, but also supremely just. And His justice requires (as He has revealed Himself in His Word) that our sins committed against His infinite majesty should be punished, not only with temporal but with eternal punishments, both in body and soul; which we cannot escape, unless satisfaction be made to the justice of God.

ARTICLE 2

Since, therefore, we are unable to make that satisfaction in our own persons, or to deliver ourselves from the wrath of God, He has been pleased of His infinite mercy to give His only begotten Son for our Surety, who was made sin, and became a curse for us and in our stead, that He might make satisfaction to divine justice on our behalf.

ARTICLE 3

The death of the Son of God is the only and most perfect sacrifice and satisfaction for sin, and is of infinite worth and value, abundantly sufficient to expiate the sins of the whole world.

ARTICLE 4

This death is of such infinite value and dignity because the Person who submitted to it was not only really man and perfectly holy, but also the only begotten Son of God, of the same eternal and infinite essence with the Father and the Holy Spirit, which qualifications were necessary to constitute Him a Savior for us; and, moreover, because it was attended with a sense of the wrath and curse of God due to us for sin.

ARTICLE 5

Moreover, the promise of the gospel is that whosoever believes in Christ crucified shall not perish, but have eternal life. This promise, together with the command to repent and believe, ought to be declared and published to all nations, and to all persons promiscuously and without distinction, to whom God out of His good pleasure sends the gospel.

ARTICLE 6

And, whereas many who are called by the gospel do not repent nor believe in Christ, but perish in unbelief, this is not owing to any defect or insufficiency in the sacrifice offered by Christ upon the cross, but is wholly to be imputed to themselves.

ARTICLE 7

But as many as truly believe, and are delivered and saved from sin and destruction through the death of Christ, are indebted for this benefit solely to the grace of God given them in Christ from everlasting, and not to any merit of their own.

ARTICLE 8

For this was the sovereign counsel and most gracious will and purpose of God the Father that the quickening and saving efficacy of the most precious death of His Son should extend to all the elect, for bestowing upon them alone the gift of justifying faith, thereby to bring them infallibly to salvation; that is, it was the will of God that Christ by the blood of the cross, whereby He confirmed the new covenant, should effectually redeem out of every people, tribe, nation, and language, all those, and those only, who were from eternity chosen to salvation and given to Him by the Father; that He should confer upon them faith, which, together with all the other saving gifts of the Holy Spirit, He purchased for them by His death; should purge them from all sin, both original and actual, whether committed before or after believing; and having faithfully preserved them even to the end, should at last bring them, free from every spot and blemish, to the enjoyment of glory in His own presence forever.

ARTICLE 9

This purpose, proceeding from everlasting love towards the elect, has from the beginning of the world to this day been powerfully accomplished, and will henceforward still continue to be accomplished, notwithstanding all the ineffectual opposition of the gates of hell; so that the elect in due time may be gathered together into one, and that there never may be wanting a Church composed of believers, the foundation of which is laid in the blood of Christ; which may steadfastly love and faithfully serve Him as its Savior (who, as a bridegroom for His bride, laid down His life for them upon the cross); and which may celebrate His praises here and through all eternity.

Rejection of Errors

The true doctrine having been explained, the Synod rejects the errors of those:

PARAGRAPH 1

Error

Who teach: That God the Father has ordained His Son to the death of the cross without a certain and definite decree to save any, so that the necessity, profitableness, and worth of what Christ merited by His death might have existed, and might remain in all its parts complete, perfect, and intact, even if the merited redemption had never in fact been applied to any person.

Refutation

For this doctrine tends to the despising of the wisdom of the Father and of the merits of Jesus Christ, and is contrary to Scripture. For thus says our Savior: *I lay down My life for the sheep, and I know them* (Jn. 10:15, 27). And the prophet Isaiah says concerning the Savior, *When You make His soul an offering for sin, He shall see His seed, He shall prolong His days, and the pleasure of the Lord shall prosper in His hand* (Isa. 53:10). Finally, this contradicts the article of faith according to which we believe the catholic Christian Church.

PARAGRAPH 2

Error

Who teach: That it was not the purpose of the death of Christ that He should confirm the new covenant of grace through His blood, but only that He should acquire for the Father the mere right to establish with man such a covenant as He might please, whether of grace or works.

Refutation

For this is repugnant to Scripture which teaches that *Jesus has become a surety of a better covenant,* and that *a testament is in force after men are dead* (Heb. 7:22; 9:15, 17).

PARAGRAPH 3

Error

Who teach: That Christ by His satisfaction merited neither salvation itself for anyone, nor faith, whereby this satisfaction of Christ unto salvation is effectually appropriated; but that He merited for the Father only the authority or the perfect will to deal again with man, and to prescribe new conditions as He might desire, obedience to which, however, depended on the free will of man, so that it therefore might have come to pass that either none or all should fulfill these conditions.

Refutation

For these adjudge too contemptuously of the death of Christ, in no wise acknowledge the most important fruit or benefit thereby gained, and bring again out of hell the Pelagian error.

PARAGRAPH 4

Error

Who teach: That the new covenant of grace, which God the Father, through the mediation of the death of Christ, made with man, does not herein consist that we by faith, inasmuch as it accepts the merits of Christ, are justified before God and saved, but in the fact that God, having revoked the demand of perfect obedience of faith, regards faith itself and the obedience of faith, although imperfect, as the perfect obedience of the law, and does esteem it worthy of the reward of eternal life through grace.

Refutation

For these contradict the Scriptures: *Being justified freely by His grace through the redemption that is in Christ Jesus; whom God set forth to be a propitiation by His blood, through faith* (Rom. 3:24–25). And these proclaim, as did the wicked Socinus, a new and strange justification of man before God, against the consensus of the whole Church.

PARAGRAPH 5

Error

Who teach: That all men have been accepted unto the state of reconciliation and unto the grace of the covenant, so that no one is worthy of condemnation on account of original sin, and that no one shall be condemned because of it, but that all are free from the guilt of original sin.

Refutation

For this opinion is repugnant to Scripture which teaches that we are *by nature children of wrath* (Eph. 2:3).

PARAGRAPH 6

Error

Who use the difference between meriting and appropriating to the end that they may instill into the minds of the imprudent and inexperienced this teaching that God, as far as He is concerned, has been minded to apply to all equally the benefits gained by the death of Christ; but that, while some obtain the pardon of sin and eternal life, and others do not, this difference depends on their own free will, which joins itself to the grace that is offered without exception, and that it is not dependent on the special gift of mercy, which powerfully works in them, that they rather than others should appropriate unto themselves this grace.

Refutation

For these, while they feign that they present this distinction in a sound sense, seek to instill into the people the destructive poison of the Pelagian errors.

PARAGRAPH 7

Error

Who teach: That Christ neither could die, nor needed to die, and also did not die, for those whom God loved in the highest degree and elected to eternal life, since these do not need the death of Christ.

Refutation

For they contradict the apostle, who declares, the Son of God *loved me, and gave Himself for me* (Gal. 2:20). Likewise, *Who shall bring a charge against God's elect? It is God who justifies; who is he who condemns? It is Christ who died* (Rom. 8:33–34), namely, for them; and the Savior who says, *I lay down My life for the sheep* (Jn. 10:15); and, *This is My commandment, that you love one another as I have loved you. Greater love has no one than this, than to lay down one's life for his friends* (Jn. 15:12–13).

The Third and Fourth Heads of Doctrine
THE CORRUPTION OF MAN, HIS CONVERSION
TO GOD, AND THE MANNER THEREOF

ARTICLE 1

Man was originally formed after the image of God. His understanding was adorned with a true and saving knowledge of his Creator, and of spiritual things; his heart and will were upright, all his affections pure, and the whole man was holy. But, revolting from God by the instigation of the devil and by his own free will, he forfeited these excellent gifts; and in the place thereof became involved in blindness of mind, horrible darkness, vanity, and perverseness of judgment; became wicked, rebellious, and obdurate in heart and will, and impure in his affections.

ARTICLE 2

Man after the fall begat children in his own likeness. A corrupt stock produced a corrupt offspring. Hence all the posterity of Adam, Christ only excepted, have derived corruption from their original parent, not by imitation, as the Pelagians of old asserted, but by the propagation of a vicious nature, in consequence of the just judgment of God.

ARTICLE 3

Therefore all men are conceived in sin, and are by nature children of wrath, incapable of saving good, prone to evil, dead in sin, and in bondage thereto; and without the regenerating grace of the Holy Spirit, they are neither able nor willing to return to God, to reform the depravity of their nature, or to dispose themselves to reformation.

ARTICLE 4

There remain, however, in man since the fall, the glimmerings of natural understanding, whereby he retains some knowledge of God, of natural things, and of the difference between good and evil, and shows some regard for virtue and for good outward behavior. But so far is this understanding of nature from being sufficient to bring him to a saving knowledge of God and to true conversion that he is incapable of using it aright even in things natural and civil. Nay further, this understanding, such as it is, man in various ways renders wholly polluted, and hinders in unrighteousness, by doing which he becomes inexcusable before God.

ARTICLE 5

Neither can the Decalogue, delivered by God to His peculiar people, the Jews, by the hands of Moses, save men. For though it reveals the greatness of sin, and more and more convinces man thereof, yet, as it neither points out a remedy nor imparts strength to extricate him from this misery, but, being weak through the flesh, leaves the transgressor under the curse, man cannot by this law obtain saving grace.

ARTICLE 6

What, therefore, neither the innate understanding nor the law could do, that God performs by the operation of the Holy Spirit through the word or ministry of reconciliation; which is the glad tidings concerning the Messiah, by means whereof it has pleased God to save such as believe, as well under the Old as under the New Testament.

ARTICLE 7

This mystery of His will God revealed to but a small number under the Old Testament; under the New Testament (the distinction between various peoples having been removed) He reveals it to many. The cause of this dispensation is not to be ascribed to the superior worth of one nation above another, nor to their better use of the innate understanding of God, but results wholly from the sovereign good pleasure and unmerited love of God. Hence they to whom so great and so gracious a blessing is communicated, above their desert, or rather notwithstanding their demerits, are bound to acknowledge it with humble and grateful hearts, and with the apostle to adore, but in no wise curiously to pry into, the severity and justice of God's judgments displayed in others to whom this grace is not given.

ARTICLE 8

As many as are called by the gospel are unfeignedly called. For God has most earnestly and truly declared in His Word what is acceptable to Him, namely, that those who are called should come unto Him. He also seriously promises rest of soul and eternal life to all who come to Him and believe.

ARTICLE 9

It is not the fault of the gospel, nor of Christ offered therein, nor of God, who calls men by the gospel and confers upon them various gifts, that those who are called by the ministry of the Word refuse to come and be converted. The fault lies in themselves; some of whom when called, regardless of their danger, reject the Word of life; others, though they receive it, suffer it not to make a lasting impression on their heart; therefore, their joy, arising only from a temporary faith, soon vanishes, and they fall away; while others choke the seed of the Word by perplexing cares and the pleasures of this world, and produce no fruit. This our Savior teaches in the parable of the sower (Matt. 13).

Article 10

But that others who are called by the gospel obey the call and are converted is not to be ascribed to the proper exercise of free will, whereby one distinguishes himself above others equally furnished with grace sufficient for faith and conversion (as the proud heresy of Pelagius maintains); but it must be wholly ascribed to God, who, as He has chosen His own from eternity in Christ, so He calls them effectually in time, confers upon them faith and repentance, rescues them from the power of darkness, and translates them into the kingdom of His own Son; that they may show forth the praises of Him who has called them out of darkness into His marvelous light, and may glory not in themselves but in the Lord, according to the testimony of the apostles in various places.

Article 11

But when God accomplishes His good pleasure in the elect, or works in them true conversion, He not only causes the gospel to be externally preached to them, and powerfully illuminates their minds by His Holy Spirit, that they may rightly understand and discern the things of the Spirit of God; but by the efficacy of the same regenerating Spirit He pervades the inmost recesses of man; He opens the closed and softens the hardened heart, and circumcises that which was uncircumcised; infuses new qualities into the will, which, though heretofore dead, He quickens; from being evil, disobedient, and refractory, He renders it good, obedient, and pliable; actuates and strengthens it, that like a good tree, it may bring forth the fruits of good actions.

Article 12

And this is that regeneration so highly extolled in Scripture, that renewal, new creation, resurrection from the dead, making alive, which God works in us without our aid. But this is in no wise effected merely by the external preaching of the gospel, by moral suasion, or such a mode of operation that, after God has performed His part, it still remains in the power of man to be regenerated or not, to be converted or to continue unconverted; but it is evidently a supernatural work, most powerful, and at the same time most delightful, astonishing, mysterious, and ineffable; not inferior in efficacy to creation or the resurrection from the dead, as the Scripture inspired by the Author of this work declares; so that all in whose heart God works in this marvelous manner are certainly, infallibly, and effectually regenerated, and do actually believe. Whereupon the will thus renewed is not only actuated and influenced by God, but in consequence of this influence becomes itself active. Wherefore also man himself is rightly said to believe and repent by virtue of that grace received.

ARTICLE 13

The manner of this operation cannot be fully comprehended by believers in this life. Nevertheless, they are satisfied to know and experience that by this grace of God they are enabled to believe with the heart and to love their Savior.

ARTICLE 14

Faith is therefore to be considered as the gift of God, not on account of its being offered by God to man, to be accepted or rejected at his pleasure, but because it is in reality conferred upon him, breathed and infused into him; nor even because God bestows the power or ability to believe, and then expects that man should by the exercise of his own free will consent to the terms of salvation and actually believe in Christ, but because He who works in man both to will and to work, and indeed all things in all, produces both the will to believe and the act of believing also.

ARTICLE 15

God is under no obligation to confer this grace upon any; for how can He be indebted to one who had no previous gifts to bestow as a foundation for such recompense? Nay, how can He be indebted to one who has nothing of his own but sin and falsehood? He, therefore, who becomes the subject of this grace owes eternal gratitude to God, and gives Him thanks forever. Whoever is not made partaker thereof is either altogether regardless of these spiritual gifts and satisfied with his own condition, or is in no apprehension of danger, and vainly boasts the possession of that which he has not. Further, with respect to those who outwardly profess their faith and amend their lives, we are bound, after the example of the apostle, to judge and speak of them in the most favorable manner; for the secret recesses of the heart are unknown to us. And as to others who have not yet been called, it is our duty to pray for them to God, who calls the things that are not as if they were. But we are in no wise to conduct ourselves towards them with haughtiness, as if we had made ourselves to differ.

ARTICLE 16

But as man by the fall did not cease to be a creature endowed with understanding and will, nor did sin which pervaded the whole race of mankind deprive him of the human nature, but brought upon him depravity and spiritual death; so also this grace of regeneration does not treat men as senseless stocks and blocks, nor take away their will and its properties, or do violence thereto; but it spiritually quickens, heals, corrects, and at the same time sweetly and powerfully bends it, that where carnal rebellion and resistance formerly prevailed, a ready and sincere spiritual obedience begins to reign; in which the true and spiritual restoration and freedom of our will consist. Wherefore, unless the admirable Author of every good work so deal with us, man can have no hope of being able to rise from his fall by his own free will, by which, in a state of innocence, he plunged himself into ruin.

ARTICLE 17

As the almighty operation of God whereby He brings forth and supports this our natural life does not exclude but require the use of means by which God, of His infinite mercy and goodness, has chosen to exert His influence, so also the aforementioned supernatural operation of God by which we are regenerated in no wise excludes or subverts the use of the gospel, which the most wise God has ordained to be the seed of regeneration and food of the soul. Wherefore, as the apostles and the teachers who succeeded them piously instructed the people concerning this grace of God, to His glory and to the abasement of all pride, and in the meantime, however, neglected not to keep them, by the holy admonitions of the gospel, under the influence of the Word, the sacraments, and ecclesiastical discipline; so even now it should be far from those who give or receive instruction in the Church to presume to tempt God by separating what He of His good pleasure has most intimately joined together. For grace is conferred by means of admonitions; and the more readily we perform our duty, the more clearly this favor of God, working in us, usually manifests itself, and the more directly His work is advanced; to whom alone all the glory, both for the means and for their saving fruit and efficacy, is forever due. Amen.

Rejection of Errors

The true doctrine having been explained, the Synod rejects the errors of those:

PARAGRAPH 1

Error

Who teach: That it cannot properly be said that original sin in itself suffices to condemn the whole human race or to deserve temporal and eternal punishment.

Refutation

For these contradict the apostle, who declares, *Therefore, just as through one man sin entered into the world, and death through sin, and thus death spread to all men, because all sinned* (Rom. 5:12); and, *The judgment which came from one offense resulted in condemnation* (Rom. 5:16); and, *The wages of sin is death* (Rom. 6:23).

PARAGRAPH 2

Error

Who teach: That the spiritual gifts or the good qualities and virtues, such as goodness, holiness, righteousness, could not belong to the will of man when he was first created, and that these, therefore, cannot have been separated therefrom in the fall.

Refutation

For such is contrary to the description of the image of God which the apostle gives in Eph. 4:24, where he declares that it consists in righteousness and holiness, which undoubtedly belong to the will.

PARAGRAPH 3

Error

Who teach: That in spiritual death the spiritual gifts are not separate from the will of man, since the will in itself has never been corrupted, but only hindered through the darkness of the understanding and the irregularity of the affections; and that, these hindrances having been removed, the will can then bring into operation its native powers, that is, that the will of itself is able to will and to choose, or not to will and not to choose, all manner of good which may be presented to it.

Refutation

This is an innovation and an error, and tends to elevate the powers of the free will, contrary to the declaration of the prophet: *The heart is deceitful above all things, and desperately wicked* (Jer. 17:9); and of the apostle: *Among whom also* (sons of disobedience) *we all once conducted ourselves in the lusts of our flesh, fulfilling the desires of the flesh and of the mind* (Eph. 2:3).

PARAGRAPH 4

Error

Who teach: That the unregenerate man is not really nor utterly dead in sin, nor destitute of all powers unto spiritual good, but that he can yet hunger and thirst after righteousness and life, and offer the sacrifice of a contrite and broken spirit, which is pleasing to God.

Refutation

For these things are contrary to the express testimony of Scripture: *You were dead in trespasses and sins* (Eph. 2:1, 5); and, *Every intent of the thoughts of his heart was only evil continually* (Gen. 6:5; 8:21). Moreover, to hunger and thirst after deliverance from misery and after life, and to offer unto God the sacrifice of a broken spirit, is peculiar to the regenerate and those that are called blessed (Ps. 51:17; Matt. 5:6).

PARAGRAPH 5

Error

Who teach: That the corrupt and natural man can so well use the common grace (by which they understand the light of nature), or the gifts still left him after the fall, that he can gradually gain by their good use a greater, that is, the evangelical or saving grace, and salvation itself; and that in this way God on His part shows Himself ready to reveal Christ unto all men, since He applies to all sufficiently and efficiently the means necessary to conversion.

Refutation

For both the experience of all ages and the Scriptures testify that this is untrue. *He declares His word to Jacob, His statutes and His judgments to Israel. He has not dealt thus with any nation; and as for His judgments, they have not known them* (Ps. 147:19–20). *Who in bygone generations allowed all nations to walk in their own ways* (Acts 14:16); and, *They* (Paul and his companions) *were forbidden by the Holy Spirit to preach the word in Asia; after they had come to Mysia, they tried to go into Bithynia, but the Spirit did not permit them* (Acts 16:6–7).

PARAGRAPH 6

Error

Who teach: That in the true conversion of man no new qualities, powers, or gifts can be infused by God into the will, and that therefore faith, through which we are first converted and because of which we are called believers, is not a quality or gift infused by God but only an act of man, and that it cannot be said to be a gift, except in respect of the power to attain to this faith.

Refutation

For thereby they contradict the Holy Scriptures, which declare that God infuses new qualities of faith, of obedience, and of the consciousness of His love into our hearts: *I will put My law in their minds, and write it on their hearts* (Jer. 31:33); and, *I will pour water on him who is thirsty, and floods on the dry ground; I will pour My Spirit on your descendents* (Isa. 44:3); and, *The love of God has been poured out in our hearts by the Holy Spirit who was given to us* (Rom. 5:5). This is also repugnant to the constant practice of the Church, which prays by the mouth of the prophet thus: *Restore me, and I will return* (Jer. 31:18).

PARAGRAPH 7

Error

Who teach: That the grace whereby we are converted to God is only a gentle advising, or (as others explain it) that this is the noblest manner of working in the conversion of man, and that this manner of working, which consists in advising, is most in harmony with man's nature; and that there is no reason why this advising grace alone should not be sufficient to make the natural man spiritual; indeed, that God does not produce the consent of the will except through this manner of advising; and that the power of the divine working, whereby it surpasses the working of Satan, consists in this that God promises eternal, while Satan promises only temporal goods.

Refutation

But this is altogether Pelagian and contrary to the whole Scripture, which, besides this, teaches yet another and far more powerful and divine manner of the Holy Spirit's working in the conversion of man, as in Ezekiel: *I will give you a new heart and put a new spirit within you; I will take the heart of stone out of your flesh and give you a heart of flesh* (Ezek. 36:26).

PARAGRAPH 8

Error

Who teach: That God in the regeneration of man does not use such powers of His omnipotence as potently and infallibly bend man's will to faith and conversion; but that all the works of grace having been accomplished, which God employs to convert man, man may yet so resist God and the Holy Spirit, when God intends man's regeneration and wills to regenerate him, and indeed that man often does so resist that he prevents entirely his regeneration, and that it therefore remains in man's power to be regenerated or not.

Refutation

For this is nothing less than the denial of all the efficiency of God's grace in our conversion, and the subjecting of the working of Almighty God to the will of man, which is contrary to the apostles, who teach that we believe *according to the exceeding greatness of His power* (Eph. 1:19); and that *God fulfills all the good pleasure of His goodness and the work of faith with power* (2 Thess. 1:11); and that *His divine power has given to us all things that pertain to life and godliness* (2 Pet. 1:3).

PARAGRAPH 9

Error

Who teach: That grace and free will are partial causes which together work the beginning of conversion, and that grace, in order of working, does not precede the working of the will; that is, that God does not efficiently help the will of man unto conversion until the will of man moves and determines to do this.

Refutation

For the ancient Church has long ago condemned this doctrine of the Pelagians according to the words of the apostle: *So then it is not of him who wills, nor of him who runs, but of God who shows mercy* (Rom. 9:16). Likewise, *For who makes you differ from another? and what do you have that you did not receive?* (1 Cor. 4:7); and, *For it is God who works in you both to will and to do for His good pleasure* (Phil. 2:13).

The Fifth Head of Doctrine
THE PERSEVERANCE OF THE SAINTS

ARTICLE 1

Those whom God, according to His purpose, calls to the communion of His Son, our Lord Jesus Christ, and regenerates by the Holy Spirit, He also delivers from the dominion and slavery of sin, though in this life He does not deliver them altogether from the body of sin and from the infirmities of the flesh.

ARTICLE 2

Hence spring forth the daily sins of infirmity, and blemishes cleave even to the best works of the saints. These are to them a perpetual reason to humiliate themselves before God and to flee for refuge to Christ crucified; to mortify the flesh more and more by the spirit of prayer and by holy exercises of piety; and to press forward to the goal of perfection, until at length, delivered from this body of death, they shall reign with the Lamb of God in heaven.

ARTICLE 3

By reason of these remains of indwelling sin, and also because of the temptations of the world and of Satan, those who are converted could not persevere in that grace if left to their own strength. But God is faithful, who having conferred grace, mercifully confirms and powerfully preserves them therein, even to the end.

ARTICLE 4

Although the weakness of the flesh cannot prevail against the power of God, who confirms and preserves true believers in a state of grace, yet converts are not always so influenced and actuated by the Spirit of God as not in some particular instances sinfully to deviate from the guidance of divine grace, so as to be seduced by and to comply with the lusts of the flesh; they must, therefore, be constant in watching and prayer, that they may not be led into temptation. When these are neglected, they are not only liable to be drawn into great and heinous sins by the flesh, the world, and Satan, but sometimes by the righteous permission of God actually are drawn into these evils. This, the lamentable fall of David, Peter, and other saints described in Holy Scripture, demonstrates.

ARTICLE 5

By such enormous sins, however, they very highly offend God, incur a deadly guilt, grieve the Holy Spirit, interrupt the exercise of faith, very grievously wound their consciences, and sometimes for a while lose the sense of God's favor, until, when they change their course by serious repentance, the light of God's fatherly countenance again shines upon them.

ARTICLE 6

But God, who is rich in mercy, according to His unchangeable purpose of election, does not wholly withdraw the Holy Spirit from His own people even in their grievous falls; nor suffers them to proceed so far as to lose the grace of adoption and forfeit the state of justification, or to commit the sin unto death or against the Holy Spirit; nor does He permit them to be totally deserted, and to plunge themselves into everlasting destruction.

ARTICLE 7

For in the first place, in these falls He preserves in them the incorruptible seed of regeneration from perishing or being totally lost; and again, by His Word and Spirit He certainly and effectually renews them to repentance, to a sincere and godly sorrow for their sins, that they may seek and obtain remission in the blood of the Mediator, may again experience the favor of a reconciled God, through faith adore His mercies, and henceforward more diligently work out their own salvation with fear and trembling.

ARTICLE 8

Thus it is not in consequence of their own merits or strength, but of God's free mercy, that they neither totally fall from faith and grace nor continue and perish finally in their backslidings; which, with respect to themselves is not only possible, but would undoubtedly happen; but with respect to God, it is utterly impossible, since His counsel cannot be changed nor His promise fail; neither can the call according to His purpose be revoked, nor the merit, intercession, and preservation of Christ be rendered ineffectual, nor the sealing of the Holy Spirit be frustrated or obliterated.

ARTICLE 9

Of this preservation of the elect to salvation and of their perseverance in the faith, true believers themselves may and do obtain assurance according to the measure of their faith, whereby they surely believe that they are and ever will continue true and living members of the Church, and that they have the forgiveness of sins and life eternal.

ARTICLE 10

This assurance, however, is not produced by any peculiar revelation contrary to or independent of the Word of God, but springs from faith in God's promises, which He has most abundantly revealed in His Word for our comfort; from the testimony of the Holy Spirit, witnessing with our spirit that we are children and heirs of God (Rom. 8:16); and lastly, from a serious and holy desire to preserve a good conscience and to perform good works. And if the elect of God were deprived of this solid comfort that they shall finally obtain the victory, and of this infallible pledge of eternal glory, they would be of all men most miserable.

ARTICLE 11

The Scripture moreover testifies that believers in this life have to struggle with various carnal doubts, and that under grievous temptations they do not always feel this full assurance of faith and certainty of persevering. But God, who is the Father of all consolation, does not suffer them to be tempted above that they are able, but will with the temptation make also the way of escape, that they may be able to endure it (1 Cor. 10:13), and by the Holy Spirit again inspires them with the comfortable assurance of persevering.

ARTICLE 12

This certainty of perseverance, however, is so far from exciting in believers a spirit of pride, or of rendering them carnally secure, that on the contrary it is the real source of humility, filial reverence, true piety, patience in every tribulation, fervent prayers, constancy in suffering and in confessing the truth, and of solid rejoicing in God; so that the consideration of this benefit should serve as an incentive to the serious and constant practice of gratitude and good works, as appears from the testimonies of Scripture and the examples of the saints.

ARTICLE 13

Neither does renewed confidence of persevering produce licentiousness or a disregard of piety in those who are recovered from backsliding; but it renders them much more careful and solicitous to continue in the ways of the Lord, which He has ordained, that they who walk therein may keep the assurance of persevering; lest, on account of their abuse of His fatherly kindness, God should turn away His gracious countenance from them (to behold which is to the godly dearer than life, and the withdrawal of which is more bitter than death) and they in consequence thereof should fall into more grievous torments of conscience.

Article 14

And as it has pleased God, by the preaching of the gospel, to begin this work of grace in us, so He preserves, continues, and perfects it by the hearing and reading of His Word, by meditation thereon, and by the exhortations, threatenings, and promises thereof, and by the use of the sacraments.

Article 15

The carnal mind is unable to comprehend this doctrine of the perseverance of the saints and the certainty thereof, which God has most abundantly revealed in His Word, for the glory of His Name and the consolation of pious souls, and which He impresses upon the hearts of the believers. Satan abhors it, the world ridicules it, the ignorant and hypocritical abuse it, and the heretics oppose it. But the bride of Christ has always most tenderly loved and constantly defended it as an inestimable treasure; and God, against whom neither counsel nor strength can prevail, will dispose her so to continue to the end. Now to this one God, Father, Son, and Holy Spirit, be honor and glory forever. Amen.

Rejection of Errors

The true doctrine having been explained, the Synod rejects the errors of those:

Paragraph 1

Error

Who teach: That the perseverance of the true believers is not a fruit of election, or a gift of God gained by the death of Christ, but a condition of the new covenant, which (as they declare) man before his decisive election and justification must fulfill through his free will.

Refutation

For the Holy Scripture testifies that this follows out of election, and is given the elect in virtue of the death, the resurrection, and intercession of Christ: *But the elect have obtained it, and the rest were hardened* (Rom. 11:7). Likewise, *He who did not spare His own Son, but delivered Him up for us all, how shall He not with Him also freely give us all things? Who shall bring a charge against God's elect? It is God who justifies; who is he who condemns? It is Christ who died, and furthermore is also risen, who is even at the right hand of God, who also makes intercession for us. Who shall separate us from the love of Christ?* (Rom. 8:32–35).

PARAGRAPH 2

Error

Who teach: That God does indeed provide the believer with sufficient powers to persevere, and is ever ready to preserve these in him if he will do his duty; but that, though all things which are necessary to persevere in faith and which God will use to preserve faith are made use of, even then it ever depends on the pleasure of the will whether it will persevere or not.

Refutation

For this idea contains an outspoken Pelagianism, and while it wishes to make men free, it makes them robbers of God's honor, contrary to the prevailing agreement of the evangelical doctrine, which takes from man all cause of boasting, and ascribes all the praise for this favor to the grace of God alone; and contrary to the apostle, who declares that it is God, *who will also confirm you to the end, that you may be blameless in the day of our Lord Jesus Christ* (1 Cor. 1:8).

PARAGRAPH 3

Error

Who teach: That the true believers and regenerate not only can fall from justifying faith and likewise from grace and salvation wholly and to the end, but indeed often do fall from this and are lost forever.

Refutation

For this conception makes powerless the grace, justification, regeneration, and continued preservation by Christ, contrary to the expressed words of the Apostle Paul: *That, while we were still sinners, Christ died for us. Much more then, having now been justified by His blood, we shall be saved from wrath through Him* (Rom. 5:8–9); and contrary to the Apostle John:

Whoever has been born of God does not sin, for His seed remains in him; and he cannot sin, because he has been born of God (1 Jn. 3:9); and also contrary to the words of Jesus Christ: *I give them eternal life, and they shall never perish; neither shall anyone snatch them out of My hand. My Father, who has given them to Me, is greater than all; and no one is able to snatch them out of My Father's hand* (Jn. 10:28–29).

PARAGRAPH 4

Error

Who teach: That true believers and regenerate can sin the sin unto death or against the Holy Spirit.

Refutation

Since the same Apostle John, after having spoken in the fifth chapter of his first epistle, verses 16 and 17, of those who sin unto death and having forbidden to pray for them, immediately adds to this in verse 18: *We know that whoever is born of God does not sin* (meaning a sin of that character), *but he who has been born of God keeps himself, and the wicked one does not touch him* (1 Jn. 5:18).

PARAGRAPH 5

Error

Who teach: That without a special revelation we can have no certainty of future perseverance in this life.

Refutation

For by this doctrine the sure comfort of the true believers is taken away in this life, and the doubts of the papist are again introduced into the Church, while the Holy Scriptures constantly deduce this assurance, not from a special and extraordinary revelation, but from the marks proper to the children of God and from the very constant promises of God. So especially the Apostle Paul declares: *No other created thing shall be able to separate us from the love of God which is in Christ Jesus our Lord* (Rom. 8:39); and John declares: *He who keeps His commandments abides in Him, and He in him. And by this we know that He abides in us, by the Spirit whom He has given us* (1 Jn. 3:24).

PARAGRAPH 6

Error

Who teach: That the doctrine of the certainty of perseverance and of salvation from its own character and nature is a cause of indolence and is injurious to godliness, good morals, prayers, and other holy exercises, but that on the contrary it is praiseworthy to doubt.

Refutation

For these show that they do not know the power of divine grace and the working of the indwelling Holy Spirit. And they contradict the Apostle John, who teaches the opposite with express words in his first epistle: *Beloved, now we are children of God; and it has not yet been revealed what we shall be, but we know that when He is revealed, we shall be like Him, for we shall see Him as He is. And everyone who has this hope in Him purifies himself, just as He is pure* (1 Jn. 3:2–3). Furthermore, these are contradicted by the example of the saints, both of the Old and the New Testament, who though they were assured of their perseverance and salvation, were nevertheless constant in prayers and other exercises of godliness.

PARAGRAPH 7

Error

Who teach: That the faith of those who believe for a time does not differ from justifying and saving faith except only in duration.

Refutation

For Christ Himself, in Matt. 13:20, Lk. 8:13, and in other places, evidently notes, besides this duration, a threefold difference between those who believe only for a time and true believers, when He declares that the former receive the seed in stony ground, but the latter in the good ground or heart; that the former are without root, but the latter have a firm root; that the former are without fruit, but that the latter bring forth their fruit in various measure, with constancy and steadfastness.

PARAGRAPH 8

Error

Who teach: That it is not absurd that one having lost his first regeneration is again and even often born anew.

Refutation

For these deny by this doctrine the incorruptibleness of the seed of God, whereby we are born again; contrary to the testimony of the Apostle Peter: *Having been born again, not of corruptible seed but incorruptible* (1 Pet. 1:23).

PARAGRAPH 9

Error

Who teach: That Christ has in no place prayed that believers should infallibly continue in faith.

Refutation

For they contradict Christ Himself, who says, *I have prayed for you (Simon), that your faith should not fail* (Lk. 22:32), and the evangelist John, who declares that Christ has not prayed for the apostles only, but also for those who through their word would believe: *Holy Father, keep through Your name those whom You have given Me*; and, *I do not pray that You should take them out of the world, but that You should keep them from the evil one* (Jn. 17:11, 15, 20).

Conclusion

And this is the perspicuous, simple, and ingenuous declaration of the orthodox doctrine respecting the five articles which have been controverted in the Belgic Churches; and the rejection of the errors, with which they have for some time been troubled. This doctrine the Synod judges to be drawn from the Word of God, and to be agreeable to the confession of the Reformed Churches. Whence it clearly appears that some, whose conduct was by no means becoming, have violated all truth, equity, and charity, in wishing to persuade the public:

[REMONSTRANT ARMINIAN VIEWS]

"*That the doctrine of the Reformed Churches concerning predestination, and the points annexed to it, by its own genius and necessary tendency, leads off the minds of men from all piety and religion; that it is an opiate administered by the flesh and the devil; and the stronghold of Satan, where he lies in wait for all, and from which he wounds multitudes, and mortally strikes through many with the darts both of despair and security; that it makes God the author of sin, unjust, tyrannical, hypocritical; that it is nothing more than an interpolated Stoicism, Manicheism, Libertinism, Turcism; that it renders men carnally secure, since they are persuaded by it that nothing can hinder the salvation of the elect, let them live as they please; and, therefore, that they may safely perpetrate every species of the most atrocious crimes; and that, if the reprobate should even perform truly all the works of the saints, their obedience would not in the least contribute to their salvation; that the same doctrine teaches that God, by a mere arbitrary act of His will, without the least respect or view to any sin, has predestinated the greatest part of the world to eternal damnation, and has created them for this very purpose; that in the same manner in which the election is the fountain and cause of faith and good works, reprobation is the cause of unbelief and impiety; that many children of the faithful are torn, guiltless, from their mother's breasts, and tyrannically plunged into hell: so that neither baptism nor the prayers of the Church at their baptism can at all profit them;*"

and many other things of the same kind which the Reformed Churches not only do not acknowledge, but even detest with their whole soul.

Wherefore, this Synod of Dort, in the name of the Lord, conjures as many as piously call upon the name of our Savior Jesus Christ to judge of the faith of the Reformed Churches, not from the calumnies which on every side are heaped upon it, nor from the private expressions of a few among ancient and modern teachers, often dishonestly quoted, or corrupted and wrested to a meaning quite foreign to their intention;

but from the public confessions of the Churches themselves, and from this declaration of the orthodox doctrine, confirmed by the unanimous consent of all and each of the members of the whole Synod.

Moreover, the Synod warns calumniators themselves to consider the terrible judgment of God which awaits them, for bearing false witness against the confessions of so many Churches; for distressing the consciences of the weak; and for laboring to render suspected the society of the truly faithful.

Finally, this Synod exhorts all their brethren in the gospel of Christ to conduct themselves piously and religiously in handling this doctrine, both in the universities and churches; to direct it, as well in discourse as in writing, to the glory of the Divine name, to holiness of life, and to the consolation of afflicted souls; to regulate, by the Scripture, according to the analogy of faith, not only their sentiments, but also their language, and to abstain from all those phrases which exceed the limits necessary to be observed in ascertaining the genuine sense of the Holy Scriptures, and may furnish insolent sophists with a just pretext for violently assailing, or even vilifying, the doctrine of the Reformed Churches.

May Jesus Christ, the Son of God, who, seated at the Father's right hand, gives gifts to men, sanctify us in the truth; bring to the truth those who err; shut the mouths of the calumniators of sound doctrine, and endue the faithful ministers of His Word with the spirit of wisdom and discretion, that all their discourses may tend to the glory of God, and the edification of those who hear them.

AMEN.

⌘

Study
Resources

⌘

HARMONY OF
THE THREE FORMS OF UNITY

❧

This "Harmony of the Confessions," based on the order of the Heidelberg Catechism, is intended to serve as an aid in locating related statements of doctrine found in the other confessions. However, each of the confessions has its own peculiar function, since each was designed to meet specific needs of the church at a given time. A harmony of the confessions can be used with profit only when the independence and integrity of each confession is respected.

HEIDELBERG CATECHISM		BELGIC CONFESSION	CANONS OF DORT
			Head & Article RE = Rejection of Errors
LD	Question	Article	
1	1	—	Head 1.12–14 • RE 1.6–7 Heads 3/4.11 • Head 5.8–12 RE 5.5
1	2	—	1.1–4
2	3	—	3/4.5–6
2	4	—	—
2	5	14–15	3/4.3–6 • 5.2–3
3	6	14	3/4.1
3	7	14–15	1.1 • 3/4.1–4
3	8	14–15, 24	3/4.3–4
4	9	14–16	1.1 • 3/4.1
4	10	15, 37	1.4 • 2.1 • 3/4.1
4	11	16–17, 20	1.1–4 • 2.1–2
5	12	20	2.1
5	13	14	2.2 • 3/4.1–4
5	14	—	—
5	15	19	2.1–4
6	16	18–21	2.1–4
6	17	19	2.1–4
6	18	10, 18–21	2.1–4
6	19	2–7	1.3 • 2.5 • 3/4.6–8

7	20	22	1.1–5 • 2.5–7 • 3/4.6
7	21	23–24	3/4.9–14 • RE 3/4.6
7	22	7	1.3 • 2.5 • 3/4.6–8
7	23	9	——
8	24	8–9	——
8	25	8–9	——
9	26	12–13	——
10	27	13	——
10	28	12–13	——
11	29	21–22	2.3
11	30	21–22, 24	2.5 • RE 2.3–6
12	31	21, 26	——
12	32	——	5.1–2
13	33	10, 18–19	——
13	34	——	——
14	35	18–19, 26	——
14	36	18–19	——
15	37	20–21	2.2–4
15	38	21	——
15	39	20–21	2.2–4
16	40	20–21	2.3–4 • RE 2.7
16	41	——	——
16	42	——	——
16	43	——	2.8
16	44	21	2.4
17	45	20	RE 5.1
18	46	26	——
18	47	19, 26	——
18	48	19, 26	——
18	49	26	——
19	50	26	——

19	51	—	2.8 • 5.1–15
19	52	37	—
20	53	11, 24	3/4.11–12 • RE 3/4.5–8 • 5.6–7
21	54	16, 27–29	1.1–18 • 2.1–9 • 5.9
21	55	28, 30–31	—
21	56	22–23	2.7–8 • 5.5
22	57	37	—
22	58	37	—
23	59	21–23	2.7–8
23	60	21–23	2.7–8
23	61	21–23	2.7–8 • RE 2.4
24	62	23–24	2.1 • 3/4.3–6 • RE 3/4.4–5
24	63	24	—
24	64	24	3/4.11 • 5.12–13 • RE 5.6
25	65	24, 33	3/4.17 • RE 3/4. 7–9 • 5.14
25	66	33	—
25	67	33	—
25	68	33	—
26	69	15, 34	—
26	70	15, 34	—
26	71	15, 24, 34	—
27	72	34	—
27	73	34	—
27	74	15, 34	1.17
28	75	35	—
28	76	35	—
28	77	35	—
29	78	35	—
29	79	35	—
30	80	35	—
30	81	35	—

30	82	35	—
31	83	29–30, 32	—
31	84	29, 32	—
31	85	29, 32	—
32	86	24	3/4.11–12 • 5.10, 12
32	87	24	—
33	88	24	3/4.11–12 • 5. 5, 7
33	89	24	3/4.11–12 • 5.5, 7
33	90	24	3/4.11–12 • 5.5, 7
33	91	24–25	—
34	92	—	—
34	93	—	—
34	94	1	—
34	95	1	—
35	96	32	—
35	97	—	—
35	98	7	3/4.17 • 5.14
36	99	—	—
36	100	—	—
37	101	36	—
37	102	—	—
38	103	—	5.14
39	104	36	—
40	105	36	—
40	106	—	—
40	107	—	—
41	108	—	—
41	109	—	—
42	110	—	—
42	111	—	—
43	112	—	—

44	113	—	—
44	114	24, 29	5.4
44	115	25	3/4.17
45	116	—	—
45	117	—	—
45	118	—	—
45	119	26	—
46	120	12–13, 26	—
46	121	13	—
47	122	2, 7	—
48	123	36–37	—
49	124	12, 24	3/4.11, 16
50	125	13	—
51	126	15, 21–23	2.7
52	127	26	5.6–8
52	128	26	—
52	129	—	—

SUMMARY OF
THE BELGIC CONFESSION
WITH SCRIPTURE TEXTS

ജ

The number of the articles of the Confession appear before the heading,
and are followed by key points and some of the Scripture texts that apply.

1. GOD AND HIS ATTRIBUTES

Spiritual—Jn. 4:24

Being—Eph. 4:6; Deut. 6:4; 1 Tim. 2:5; 1 Cor. 8:6

Eternal—Deut. 33:27; Isa. 40:28

Incomprehensible—Rom. 11:33

Invisible—Rom. 1:20; 1 Tim. 1:17

Immutable—Ps. 102:27; Mal. 3:6; Heb. 13:8; James 1:17

Infinite—1 Kg. 8:27; Ps. 147: 5; Isa. 44:6; Jer. 23:24

Almighty—Gen. 17:1; Deut. 32:39; 1 Sam. 14:6; 1 Chr. 29:11–12; 2 Chr. 20:6; Job 34:14; Ps. 115:3; 135:6; Isa. 26:4; Mk. 14:36; Rev. 19:1,6

Perfectly wise—Ps. 104:24; Dan. 2:20–22; Rom. 16:27; 1 Tim. 1:17

Just—Jer. 12:1; Job 34:10–12; Zeph. 3:5; Rom. 3:4–6, 26; 1 Jn. 1:9; Rev. 16:5–7

Good—Ex. 34:6; Ps. 25:8; 86:5; 145:7; Matt. 19:17; Rom. 11:22

Fountain of all good—1 Chr. 29:10–12; 2 Chr. 5:13; Ps. 33:5; 107:8–9, 43; James 1:17

2. GOD REVEALS HIMSELF TO MAN

By creation, preservation, and government of the universe—Ps. 19:2; Rom. 1:19, 20; Eph. 4:6

By the written Word—Ps. 19:8; 1 Cor. 12:6

3. THE NATURE OF THE WORD OF GOD

Inspired by God—2 Pet. 1:21

God inspired the prophets—Ex. 24:4; Ps. 102:19; Hab. 2:2

God inspired the apostles—Gal. 1:8–12; 2 Tim. 3:16; Rev. 1:11

God wrote with His own finger—Ex. 31:18

4. THE CANON OF THE OLD AND NEW TESTAMENTS

Thirty-Nine (39) Old Testament books

Twenty-Seven (27) New Testament books

5. THESE ARE AUTHORIZED BY GOD, NOT THE CHURCH

2 Tim. 3:14–17; 2 Pet. 1:19–21

6. CANON VS. THE APOCRYPHAL BOOKS

7. THE SUFFICIENCY OF SCRIPTURE

Sufficient for salvation—Rom. 15:4; Jn. 4:25; 2 Tim. 3:15–17; 1 Pet. 1:1

The Scriptures may not be perverted—1 Pet. 4:11; 1 Cor. 15:2, 3; Gal. 1:8, 9; Rom. 15:4; 1 Tim. 1:3; 2 Tim. 3:14; I1 Jn. 10; Acts 26:22

We may not add to or subtract from the Scriptures—Deut. 12:32; Prov. 30:6; Jn. 4:25; Rev. 22:18

The Scriptures may not be compared to the word of man—Ps. 62:9, 10; Isa. 1:12; Matt. 15:3; 17:5; Mk. 7:7; Rom. 3:4; 1 Cor. 2:4; 2 Tim. 4:3, 4

Anything not in agreement with Scripture must be rejected—Gal. 1:7–10; 6:16; Rom. 1:18; 2 Thess. 2:2, 3, 9–12; 1 Jn. 4:1; 2 Jn. 10; 3 Jn. 10, 11; Jude 3, 4

8. GOD IS TRIUNE (THREE IN ONE)

One in essence—Deut. 6:4; 1 Kg. 8:60; Isa. 43:10; 44:6; 45:18; Mk. 12:29; Jn. 17:3; James 2:19

Three eternally distinct persons—Gen. 1:26; Gen. 3:22; Isa. 6:3, 8; Matt. 28:19; 2 Cor. 13:14; Gal. 4:4, 6; 2 Thess. 2:13–16; Jn. 17:21; 1 Pet. 1:2

God the Father—the Creator—Gen. 1:1; Deut. 4:32; 1 Cor. 8:6; Col. 1:16

God the Son—the Word—Jn. 1:1, 2; Rev. 19:13; 1 Jn. 1:1

The Son is wisdom—Lk. 2:40, 46–47

The Son is the image of the Father—Col 1:15; Heb. 1:3

God the Holy Spirit—the eternal power and might—Gen. 1:2; Matt. 12:28; Rom. 8:11; 1 Cor. 2:4–5, 10–11; proceeding from the Father and the Son—Jn. 14:26; 15:26; 16:7; Gal. 4:6

The Trinity is not divided or intermixed—Phil 2:6–7; Gal. 4:4; Jn. 1:14; 10:30, 38; 14:10–11

9. PROOFS FOR THE DOCTRINE OF THE TRINITY FROM THE SCRIPTURES

Gen. 1:26, 27; 3:22; Matt. 3:16–17; 28:19; Lk. 1:35; 2 Cor. 13:13; Ps.

45:8; Isa. 61:1; Eccl. 12:3; Mal. 2:10; 1 Pet. 1:2; 1 Jn. 1:7; 4:14; 1 Cor. 6:11; Gal. 4:6; Tit. 3:5; Rom. 8:9; Jn. 14:16

10. JESUS CHRIST IS TRUE GOD

Begotten from eternity, not created—Jn. 1:1–3, 14, 18, 49; Jn. 8:58; Col. 1:15; Heb. 1:5–8

Co-essential (of the same Being as the Father and the Holy Spirit)—Jn. 10:30; Phil. 2:6; Heb. 1:3

Co-eternal with the Father and the Holy Spirit—Jn. 1:2; 17:5; Heb. 7:3; Rev. 1:8; Mic. 5:2

Active in the creation—Jn. 1:3; Heb. 1:2; Col. 1:16

11. THE HOLY SPIRIT IS TRUE GOD

Sent by the Father Ps. 33:6, 17; Jn. 14:26; 15:26; and the Son—Jn. 16:7; Gal. 4:6; Rom. 8:9

The Holy Spirit is true and eternal God—Gen. 1:2; Isa. 48:16; 61:6; Acts 5:3, 4; 28:25; 1 Cor. 3:16; 6:19; Ps. 139:7

12. THE DOCTRINE OF CREATION

God created all things of nothing for His own pleasure—Gen. 1:1; Ps. 115:5; 148:5–6; Isa. 14:24–27; 40:26; Jn. 1:3; 1 Cor. 8:6; Col. 1:16; Heb. 3:4; Rev. 4:11

God upholds and governs all things—Heb. 1:3; Ps. 104:10; Acts 17:25

For the service of mankind—1 Tim. 4:3–4; Rom. 8:28; Gen. 1:29–30; 9:2–3; Ps. 37:24–26; 55:22; 104:14–15; 145:15–20; Matt. 6:8, 25–26; 7:9–10; Acts 14:17

That man may serve God—1 Cor. 3:22; 6:20; Eph. 2:10; Matt. 4:10

God created the angels—Col 1:16; Matt. 25:31

To be His messengers—Ps 34:7; 103:30; 148:2; Matt. 1:20; 2:13; Lk. 1:26–38; 2:9–12; Rev. 1: 20ff.

To serve His elect people—Gen. 24:7, 40; Ex. 23:20; 1 Kg. 19:5–8; Ps. 34:7; 91:11–12; Dan. 7:10; Matt. 24:31ff. Lk. 16:22; Acts 12:7–10; Heb. 1:7, 17; Rev. 5:11ff.

Some have fallen into everlasting perdition—Jn. 8:44; 2 Pet. 2:4; Lk. 8:31; Jude 6; Rev. 12:3–9

They are the enemies of God—1 Pet. 5:8; Job 1:7;

They are the enemies of the Church—Gen. 3:1ff; Matt. 13:25; 2 Cor. 2:11; 11:3, 14; 1 Pet. 5:8; Rev. 12:17

They are condemned and await judgment—Gen. 3:15; Matt. 25:41; Lk. 8:30–31; Rev. 12:8–10

13. GOD PROVIDENTIALLY CARES FOR HIS CREATION

God rules over all according to His holy will—Jn. 5:17; Acts 17:25–26; Heb. 1:3; Prov. 16:1–4; Ps. 104:9ff.; 139:2ff.

Nothing comes by chance, but by God's appointment only—James 4:15; Job 1:21; 1 Kg. 22:20; Acts 4:28; 13:48; 1 Sam. 2:25; Ps. 45:7; 105:25; 115:3; Amos 3:6; Deut. 19:5; Prov. 21:1; Isa. 10:57; 46:9, 10; 2 Thess. 2:11; Ezek. 14:9; Rom. 1:28; Acts 2:23; Gen. 45:8; 50:20; 2 Sam. 16:10; Gen. 27:20; Ps. 75:7, 8; Isa. 45:7; Lam. 3:37–38; 1 Kg. 22:34, 38; Ex. 21:13; etc.

God is just, even when men and the devil act unjustly—Job 34:10–19; Ps. 7:9, 11; 11:4–5, 7; 145:17; Eccl. 3:15–17; Isa. 31:2; 61:8; Jer. 11:20; Nahum 1:3, 6; Zeph. 3:5; Matt. 8:31–32; Jn. 3:8; Acts 2:23–24; Rom. 2:2–11; 3:4–6; 3:26; 11:22; 2 Cor. 10:13; 2 Tim. 2:13; 2 Pet. 2:9; Rev. 16:5–7; 19:2

God's ways are beyond understanding, but not beyond belief—Isa. 55:8–11; Rom. 9:20–23; 11:33–36; Heb. 11:1, 3

God watches over us with a fatherly care and power—Gen. 39:2–3; 1 Kg. 17:1–7, 9; Job. 1:12; 2:6; Dan. 3:17, 25; 6:22; Matt. 6:30–32; Matt. 7:9–11; 10:29–30; 24:22; Lk. 18:7–8; 21:18

14. MAN—HIS CREATION, FALL, AND DEPRAVITY

Created in the image of God—Gen. 1:26, 27; 9:6; Eph. 4:24; Col. 3:10

Created good, righteous, and able to obey God—Gen. 1:31; Eccl. 7:29; 1 Cor. 11:7

He did not understand His excellency—Ps. 8:3–9; 49:20

He listened to the devil—Gen. 3:6, 17; Jn. 8:43–45

He transgressed the command of life and separated himself from God—Gen. 2:16–17; 3:6–7; Isa. 59:2; Rom. 3:23; Eph. 2:12

Man's entire nature became corrupt—Gen. 6:5; Rom. 3:10–20; Eph. 2:1; 4:17–19

Man came under the curse and punishment of physical and spiritual death—Gen. 2:17; 3:19–24; Rom. 5:12; Eph. 2:1–3; Col. 2:13; Ps. 51:5; 58:3

He is left without excuse—Rom. 1:20–21; 3:19;

The light within man is changed to darkness—Eph. 4:18; 5:8; Matt. 6:23; Jn. 1:5; Rom. 1:20–32

Man's free will is lost—he is now a slave to sin—Gen. 6:5; Isa. 26:12; Ps. 94:11; Jn. 6:44, 65; 8:34, 47; 10:25–26; Rom. 6:16–17, 20–21; 7:5, 17

Man has nothing unless it is given him by God—Jn. 3:27; Isa. 26:12

He cannot come to God unless God draws him—Jn. 5:40; 6:44, 65;

Rom. 3:11; Eph. 2:13

The carnal will is at enmity with God—Rom. 8:7–8; James 4:4

Man's knowledge is corrupted—Gen. 6:5; 8:21; Ps. 94:11; Eccl. 9:3; Jer. 17:9; Rom. 3:11; 1 Cor. 2:14; 2 Pet. 3:5ff.

Man is unable to do any good except by the power of God—2 Cor. 3:5; Rom. 7:18–25; Phil 2:13; Jn. 15:5

15. THE DOCTRINE OF ORIGINAL SIN

It extends to all of mankind—Rom. 5:12, 13; Ps. 51:5; Rom. 3:10; Gen. 6:3; Jn. 3:6; 1 Kg. 8:46; 2 Chron. 6:36; Ps. 130:3; Prov. 20:9; Eccl. 7:20, 29; Isa. 53:6; 64:6

Children are conceived and born in sin—Ps. 51:5; 58:3; Isa. 48:8; Rom. 5:12, 14, 18

Original sin produces all sorts of sin—Mark 7:21–23; Gal. 5:19–21; Rom. 1:21–32; 3:10–20; 7:8, 10, 13, 17–20; Eph. 4:17–19

It brings condemnation to all men—Rom. 5:18; 6:16; Eph. 2:3, 5

By grace and mercy alone man's sin is forgiven—Rom. 5:17–19; Eph. 2:4–9

Man may not rest contented, but must desire to be delivered from the body of this death—Rom. 6:3, 19; 7:18, 24; Col. 3:1–5

16. THE DOCTRINE OF ETERNAL ELECTION

God reveals Himself to be merciful and just—Rom. 3:24–26; Eph. 2:4–5

God is merciful in choosing some to salvation in Christ without respect to their works—Rom. 9:9–16; 18, 22–23; 3:12; 11:5–6, 32; Eph. 1:4–5; 2:8–10; Ps. 100:3; 1 Jn. 4:10; Deut. 7:7–8; 32:8–9; 1 Sam. 12:22; Ps. 65:5; Mal. 1:2; 2 Tim. 1:9; 2:19; Rom. 8:29; Titus 3:4–5; Acts 2:47; 13:48; 1 Pet. 1:2; Jn. 6:27; 15:16; 19:9

God is just in leaving sinners in their condemnation—Rom. 9:17–18; Matt. 24:40–41

God's election is unconditional (not with respect to man's works)—Rom. 9:11–13, 16; 2 Tim. 1:9; Rom. 10:20; 1 Cor. 1:27–29

17. MAN'S RECOVERY AFTER THE FALL

Man fled, but God sought him out—Gen. 3:8–9, 19; Isa. 65:1–2

God would send His Son to save man and punish Satan—Heb. 2:14; Gen. 3:15; 22:18; Isa. 7:14; Jn. 7:42; 2 Tim. 2:8; Heb. 7:14; Gal. 4:4; Matt. 25:41

18. THE PERSON AND WORK OF JESUS CHRIST, THE INCARNATE SON OF GOD

Foretold by the prophets—Isa. 11:1; Lk. 1:55; Gen. 26:4; 2 Sam. 7:12; Ps. 132:11; Isa. 53; Acts 13:23

Became a man in the form of a servant—1 Tim. 2:5; 3:16; Jn. 13:5ff.; Isa. 52:13–53:12; Phil. 2:7

A true human nature, sin excepted—Heb. 2:14–15; 4:15

Conceived by the Holy Spirit, born of the virgin Mary—Lk. 1:31, 34–35, 42; Gal. 4:4; Heb. 2:16, 17; Isa. 7:14; Matt. 1:23

   He had a body and soul as a real man—Matt. 26:38; Jn. 12:27

   Of the flesh and blood of man—Heb. 2:14

   Of the true seed of David—Matt. 1:1–17; Acts 2:30; Ps. 132:11; Rom. 1:3

   The fruit of the womb of the virgin Mary—Luke 1:42

   Made of a woman—Gal. 4:4

   A branch of David—Jer. 33:15

   A shoot of the root of Jesse—Isa. 11:1

   Of the tribe of Judah—Gen. 49:10; Heb. 7:14; Matt. 1:2; Lk. 2:4–5; 3:33

   Descended from the Jews according to the flesh—Rom. 9:5

   Of the seed of Abraham—Matt. 1:1, 17; Gen. 22:18; 2 Sam. 7:12; Gal. 3:16

   Like unto His brethren, sin excepted—Heb. 2:15–17

   He is Immanuel, God with us—Isa. 7:14; Matt. 1:23

19. CHRIST IS ONE PERSON WITH TWO DISTINCT NATURES—DIVINE AND HUMAN—VERY GOD AND VERY MAN

His divine nature is eternal—Heb. 7:3; Jn. 1:13; 8:56–58; Col 1:17

His human nature had a beginning; remained finite—1 Cor. 15:13, 21; Phil. 3:21; Matt. 26:11; Acts 1:2, 11; 3:21; Lk. 24:39; Jn. 1:14; 20:25, 27; Gal. 4:4

At death His soul went to His Father, yet His divine nature remained with His body—Lk. 23:46; Matt. 27:50

20. IN CHRIST IS THE JUSTICE AND MERCY OF GOD REVEALED

God's justice is seen in that sin is punished in Christ as our iniquities were laid upon Him—Isa. 53:6; Jn. 1:29; Rom. 8:3, 32–33; 2 Cor. 5:19–21;

Heb. 2:14; 1 Jn. 4:9

God's mercy is seen in the resurrection from the dead through which we may obtain immortality and life—Rom. 4:25; 8:11; 1 Cor. 15:17–22; 55–57; 1 Thess. 4:14–18

21. CHRIST IS OUR HIGH PRIEST AND ONLY SATISFACTION FOR SIN

An everlasting high priest, after the order of Melchizedek—Ps. 110:4; Heb. 5:10; 7:15–17

He presented Himself as a sacrifice to fully satisfy God's justice for our sins—Col. 1:14; 2:14; Rom. 5:8–9; Heb. 2:17; 9:14; Rom. 3:24; 8:2; Jn. 3:16; 15:3; Acts 2:24; 13:28; 1 Tim. 2:6; Isa. 53; 1 Jn. 2:2; 4:10

He was condemned by Pontius Pilate—Lk. 23:22, 24; Matt. 27:24; Acts 4:27–28; 13:28; Ps. 22:16; 69:5; Jn. 18:38; 1 Pet. 3:18

He restored that which He took not away—Ps. 69:5

He suffered, the just for the unjust—1 Pet. 3:18; Lk. 22:44; 1 Pet. 1:18–21

He suffered the hell of being forsaken by God—Ps. 22:2; Matt. 27:46

Faith in Christ crucified alone brings salvation and comfort—1 Cor. 2:2; Phil. 3:8; Heb. 9:25, 26; 10:14; Matt. 12:28–30; Rom. 3:22, 24–26; 5:1–2; Eph. 2:8–9; Matt. 1:21; Acts 4:12

22. BELIEVERS ARE JUSTIFIED BY FAITH IN JESUS CHRIST

True faith is begun in our hearts by the Holy Spirit—Eph. 3:16–17; Jn. 3:38; Ps. 51:13; Eph. 1:17–18; 1 Cor. 2:10–14; 12:3; Titus 3:5

True faith seeks nothing beside Christ and Him crucified—1 Cor. 2:2; Acts 4:12; Gal. 2:20–21; Jer. 23:6; 31:10; 1 Cor. 1:30; 3:11; Jn. 6:68–69

True faith in Jesus Christ means complete salvation—any hope in works as meritorious is blasphemy—Matt. 1:21; Rom. 3:27; 8:1, 33; 10:6; Gal. 2:6; 1 Pet. 1:4–5; Eph. 2:8–9; Col 2:10

True faith itself is not a meritorious work and does not justify us, but it is the instrument by which Christ becomes our righteousness—Gal. 3:22; Rom. 4:16; Jer. 23:6; 1 Cor. 1:30; Eph. 2:8–9; 2 Tim. 1:2; 3:9; Lk. 1:77; Rom. 3:22–25; 4:5; 5:1–2; Ps. 32:1–2; Phil. 3:9; Titus 3:5

23. JUSTIFICATION CONSISTS IN THE FORGIVENESS OF SINS AND THE IMPUTATION OF CHRIST'S RIGHTEOUSNESS

Salvation comes by the remission of sins in Christ, in whom we have righteousness imputed to us without our works—Lk. 1:77; Col. 1:14; Ps. 32:1–2; Rom. 3:21–25; 4:4–7; Titus 3:5; Acts 13:38–39; 2 Cor. 5:19, 21; Phil 3:9; Gal. 3:2–3, 11

We are justified freely by grace—Rom. 3:23; 5:17, 18; 9:30–33; Acts 4:12; Gal. 3:11

All glory for salvation belongs to God—Ps. 115:1; 1 Cor. 4:7; Rom. 4:2; 11:36; 16:25–27; 1 Cor. 2:4–5; Matt. 6:24; Gal. 6:14; Phil. 2:10–11; Rev. 7:12

All trust in ourselves must be gone—Prov. 3:5; 1 Cor. 4:7; Rom 4:2; 1 Cor. 1:29, 31

> We must rely on the obedience of Christ crucified alone—Rom. 5:19; 10:4; 1 Cor. 1:30; Phil. 2:8; 3:9; Heb. 10:13

> Christ's obedience becomes ours through faith in Him—Heb. 11:6–7; Eph. 2:8; 2 Cor. 5:19; 1 Tim. 2:6; Rom. 4:16, 22–24; 5:19; Gal. 3:22

Being justified and made righteous we have confidence to come before God—Rom. 5:1; Eph. 2:13; 3:12; Heb. 10:17–25; 1 Jn. 2:1

> Coming to God any other way would consume us—Isa. 33:14; Deut. 27:26; James 2:10; Matt. 22:11–14

> In ourselves no man can be justified—Ps. 130:3; 143:2; Matt. 7:21–23; 18:23–26; Lk. 16:15; Rom. 3:20; Gal. 3:11

24. OUR SANCTIFICATION AND GOOD WORKS

Faith comes by the hearing of the Word of God and the work of the Holy Spirit—1 Pet. 1:23; 1 Cor. 2:14; Rom. 10:17; Jn. 5:24; Jn. 3:5; I Thess 1:5; 2 Tim. 1:13, 14; Titus 3:5–6

Being regenerated, we are new creatures—2 Cor. 5:17; Rom. 8:15; Jn. 6:29; Col. 2:12; 3:1–10; Phil 1:1, 29; Eph. 2:8, 10

> We are free from the bondage of sin—Acts 15:9; Rom. 6:4, 14; Phil. 3:7–14; Titus 2:12; Gal. 4:3–5; 5:1; Jn. 8:36

> It is impossible that the believer would not live a holy life because he is justified by faith—Matt. 7:18; Rom. 6:1–2; Jn. 15:5; Gal. 5:1, 13; Eph. 2:8–10; 4:22–24; Col 2:6–7; 3:9–10; Titus 3:8; James 2:17–20; 2 Pet. 1:2–4; 1 Jn. 3:8–10; 5:18

> Faith is never empty, but works by love—Titus 3:8; Jn. 15:5,12; Heb. 11:6; 1 Tim. 1:5; Gal. 5:6, 13; Rom. 6:16–22; 12:1–2; 1 Jn. 3:16–18; 4:7–8; 5:1–3; James 2:14–17, 26; 1 Cor. 13

Our works are sanctified by God's grace, but they do not merit our justification—2 Tim. 1:9; Rom. 9:32; Titus 3:5

> We are justified by faith before we do good works—Rom. 4:4; Gen. 4:4; Rom. 11:6; Eph. 2:8–10

> Only if the tree is good can the fruits produced be good—Jn. 15:5–6; Matt. 7:17–18; Heb. 11:6; Rom. 14:23;

> We are indebted to God for our good works, not He to us—1 Cor. 4:7; Isa. 26:12; Gal. 3:5; 1 Thess. 2:13; Eph. 2:10

God works in us to will and do His pleasure—Phil. 2:12–13; Heb. 13:20–21

When we have accomplished something, we must still say we are unprofitable servants—we have only done our duty, not more—Luke 17:10

God rewards our good works out of His grace—Matt. 10:42; 25:34–35; Rev. 3:12, 21; Rom. 11:6; 2:6; 2 Jn. 8

We do not base our salvation on these works—Eph. 2:8–10

We can do no perfect work, but they are all polluted by the flesh—Isa. 64:6; James 2:10; Phil. 2:20; 1 Jn. 1:8–10; Rom. 7:14, 15; Eccl. 7:20

If we did not rely totally on the merits of Christ, our consciences could not rest—Isa. 28:16; Rom. 10:11; Hab. 2:4; Heb. 9:9; 10:2, 22; 1 Pet. 3:15–16, 21

25. THE CEREMONIAL LAW IS ABOLISHED

Ceremonies and figures of the law ceased with the coming of Christ Gal. 5:2–6; Col. 2:14–15, 17; Heb. 10:1

Ceremonial laws must be abolished by Christians—Gal. 3:1; 4:9–11; 5:2–4; Col. 2:16–17; Heb.9:9–14; 9:24–25; 10:4, 8–14

The law is fulfilled in Christ—Matt. 5:17; Rom. 10:4; Heb. 10:19–22

26. JESUS CHRIST IS THE ONLY INTERCESSOR BETWEEN GOD AND MAN

We have only one Mediator and Advocate—Jesus Christ—1 Tim. 2:5; 1 Jn. 2:1; Rom. 8:33

We must not be afraid of the majesty of Jesus or seek another—Jer. 2:13, 33; Jn. 6:68–69; Heb. 2:17; 4:14–16; 10:19–22; 13:5–6

No one loves us more than Jesus—Jn. 10:11–14; 1 Jn. 4:10; Rom. 5:8; Eph. 3:18–19

All power and majesty belong to Jesus who sits at the right hand of God. Matt. 11:27; 28:18; Mk. 16:19; Rom. 8:33; Eph. 1:19–23; Col. 3:1

The saints never practiced nor required the calling on the saints as mediators—Acts 10:25–26; 4:12–15; 1 Tim. 2:5; Heb. 8:6; 9:15, 24; 12:24

We may not plead our unworthiness as a reason for not approaching Christ, because we come only because of the worthiness of Jesus Christ—Dan. 9:17–18; Jn. 16:23; Gal. 2:16; Eph. 2:8–9, 18; 3:12; Phil. 3:9; Acts 4:12; 1 Cor. 1:31; Titus 3:5; Heb. 10:19–20

Jesus perfectly understands our temptations—Heb. 2:17–18; 4:14–16; 10:19–22

His priesthood is unchanging—Heb. 7:24–25

Jesus is the only way we can come to the Father—Jn. 14:6

We may not seek another advocate, since God appointed His own Son—Ps. 44:21; 1 Tim. 2:5; 1 Jn. 2:1; Rom. 8:33; Jn. 13:13–14; 14:13; 16:23

27. WE BELIEVE IN ONE HOLY CATHOLIC CHURCH— THE ASSEMBLY OF ALL TRUE CHRISTIAN BELIEVERS

This one Church is from the beginning to the end of the world—2 Sam. 7:16; Ps. 46:5; 102:14; Isa. 2:2; Jer. 31:36; Matt. 28:20; Eph. 1:4; 3:21

Christ is the eternal King of the Church—Matt. 16:18; Lk. 1:32; Lk. 17:21; Isa. 9:6–7; 11:10; Eph. 1:20–22; Phil. 2:9–11; Heb. 2:9; Rev. 19:16

God preserves and supports the Church—Matt. 16:18; Jn. 16:33; Gen. 22:17; Jn. 10:29; 2 Tim. 2:19; Lk. 12:32; 17:21; Rom. 8:35–39; 9:29; 11:2, 4; 12:4; 1 Kg. 19:18; Titus 1:2

The Church is dispersed throughout all the world, yet is united in one faith and spirit—Acts 4:32; Eph. 4:3–4; 1 Cor. 12:12–14

28. ALL MEN ARE DUTYBOUND TO JOIN THE TRUE CHURCH

Outside the holy catholic Church there is no salvation—Joel 2:32; Jn. 6:67–68; Acts 4:11–12; 1 Pet. 3:20

No person should separate himself from the true Church—Isa. 52:11; Acts 2:40; 1 Cor. 12:15–25

Unity must be maintained in the Church—Ps. 22:23; Eph. 4:3, 12; 1 Cor. 1:10–13; 3:36; 12:25; Heb. 2:12

Believers must submit to its doctrine and discipline—Ps. 2:10–12; Matt. 11:29; 18:15–18; Acts 15:5–6, 24–29; Rom. 6:17; 16:17; 1 Tim. 1:18–20; 3:15; 2 Tim. 4:3; Heb. 13:17

Members must serve one another with the talents God has given them— Eph. 4:11–13; 1 Cor. 12:12ff.; Phil 2:4–6

Men must separate themselves in a spiritual sense from those who do not belong to the Church—Acts 2:40; Isa. 52:11; 1 Cor. 5:1–13; 2 Cor. 6:14–17; Gal. 1:8–10; 1 Jn. 2:15–17; 2 Jn. 10–11; 3 Jn. 10–11; Jude 18–23; Rev. 18:4

Believers must join the Church wherever God establishes it without regard for persecution of the unbelieving world—Matt. 5:10–12; 10:16–23; 12:30; 24:8–10; Mk. 13:13; Lk. 6:22–23; Jn. 15:18–19; Isa. 49:22; Dan. 3:17–18; 6:8–10; Acts 4:17, 19; 17:17; 18:13; 2 Cor. 4:8–12; 6:4–10; 11:23–27; 12:10; Gal. 4:29; 2 Tim. 3:12; Heb. 11:24–27; 12:3; 13:13; 1 Pet. 4:12–16; Rev. 14:14; 17:14

29. THE MARKS OF THE TRUE CHURCH DISTINGUISH IT FROM THE FALSE SECTS

The pure doctrine of the Gospel is preached—Jn. 8:47; 10:27; Eph. 2:20;

Acts 17:11–12; 20:27–28; Gal. 1:6–8; Col. 1:23; 1 Tim. 1:3–11; 2:7–8; 4:6–11; 2 Tim. 3:13–17; 4:2–5; 1 Cor. 1:18, 21; 2:1–2; Titus 1:9; 2:1ff.; 1 Pet. 5:2; 2 Jn. 9

The pure administration of the sacraments instituted by Christ—Matt. 28:19; Lk. 22:19, 29; 1 Cor. 11:23–30

The faithful use of church discipline in punishing sinners—Matt. 18:15–18; 1 Cor. 5:1–8, 11; 2 Thess. 3:14–15; 2 Jn. 10–11

Jesus Christ must be acknowledged to be the only Head of the Church—Eph. 1:22–23; Jn. 10:4–5, 14; Rev. 19:16

The members must be willing to bear the marks of Christians, by faith—Jn. 17:20; Gal. 6:17; Eph. 1:13; 2 Thess. 1:4; 2 Tim. 1:8, 12; 2:9–12; 4:16–17; 1 Pet. 3:14–17; 4:3–19; Rev. 12:11

Receive Jesus as the only Savior—Acts 4:11–12; 1 Jn. 4:2

Avoid sin and follow after righteousness—Isa. 51:1; 1 Jn. 3:8–10; Acts 10:35; Phil. 1:10–11; 3:13–19; 2 Thess. 5:15; 1 Tim. 6:11; 2 Tim. 2:22; Heb. 12:14; 3 Jn. 11

Love God and our neighbor—Matt. 22:37–40; Gal. 5:13–14; James 2:8–9; 1 Jn. 3:10–14; 4:10–11, 19–21; 5:1–3

Fight against the infirmities of the flesh through the Spirit—Rom. 6:12–13; 7:6, 17ff.; 8:9–13, 26; Gal. 5:17ff.; 2 Tim. 4:7–8; Jude 3

The false church finds more authority in herself than in the Word of God—Num. 15:39; Deut. 12:32; Isa. 29:13; Matt. 15:9; Titus 1:10–16; Col 2:18–23; 3:8, 18–23; Ps. 2:3; Rev. 12:4; 17:3–4, 6; Jn. 16:1, 2; 2 Tim. 3:14–17

30. THE GOVERNMENT AND OFFICERS OF THE CHURCH

The minister must preach the Word and administer the sacraments—Eph. 4:11; Jn. 20:23; 1 Cor. 4:1; 2 Cor. 5:20; Acts 26:17, 18; Lk. 10:16; 1 Tim. 4:14–16; 5:17, 18; 2 Tim. 1:6; 2:15; 4:2–5; Acts 6:2, 4; 1 Cor. 2:1–5; 11:23ff.

Elders and deacons, with the minister, form the consistory of the church—Acts 6:3; 14:23

> To propagate true doctrine and punish transgressors—Matt. 18:17; 1 Cor. 5:4–5; 1 Tim. 3:1–15; Titus 1:5–11; Acts 20:28–30

> These men must be chosen according to the rule of Paul to Timothy—1 Tim. 3:1–13; Titus 1:5–16; Acts 6:1–7

31. MINISTERS, ELDERS, AND DEACONS SHOULD BE ELECTED BY THE CHURCH, NOT APPOINTED BY SOMEONE OUTSIDE THE CONGREGATION

Acts 6:3; 1 Tim. 4:12–16; 5:22; Acts 14:23

They must wait until it pleases God to call them by the people—Jer. 23:21; Heb. 5:4; Acts 1:23; 8:18–22; 13:2; 2 Tim. 1:6–7; 2:2

Ministers of the Word have equal powers wherever they are, under Christ—1 Cor. 4:1–4; 2 Cor. 5:20; Acts 26:16–17; 1 Tim. 4:12; 1 Pet. 5:1–4

Jesus Christ is the only Head of the Church—1 Pet. 2:4–8, 25; 5:4; Eph. 1:22; Col. 1:18

Ministers and elders ought to be regarded highly for their work's sake—1 Thess. 5:12–13; 1 Tim. 5:17; Heb. 13:17

32. ORDER AND DISCIPLINE IN THE CHURCH

Ordinances for the government of the church should be instituted if they are in accordance with the teachings of Christ—Col. 2:6, 7; 1 Cor. 7:6, 10, 12

All inventions of man introduced which bind and compel the conscience are forbidden—Isa. 29:13; Matt. 15:9; Gal. 5:1; Rom. 14:13–15:2; 16:17–18; 1 Cor. 7:23; 8:9–13; Col. 2:18–23; 3:23–24

Excommunication or church discipline is required to maintain unity and purity—Matt. 18:17; 1 Cor. 5:5; 1 Tim. 1:20

33. THE SACRAMENTS

Ordained of God to seal His promises and be pledges of the grace of God—Gen. 9:13–15; 17:9–14; Ex. 12:14, 43–50; Rom. 4:11

Christ must be the object in them—Col. 2:11, 17; 1 Cor. 5:7

Christ has instituted only two sacraments—Holy Baptism and the Holy Supper—Matt. 26:36; 28:19

34. HOLY BAPTISM

Christ instituted baptism after abolishing circumcision—Col. 2:11–12; 1 Pet. 3:21; 1 Cor. 10:2; Gal. 5:6

Baptism is to be in the name of the Triune God—Father, Son, and Holy Spirit—Matt. 28:19; Acts 18:25; 19:3–5

The water sprinkled represents the sprinkling of the blood of Jesus which cleanses us from all sin—1 Cor. 6:11; Titus 3:5; Heb. 9:13–14; 12:24; 1 Jn. 1:7; Rev. 1:6

Not the water, but the blood of Christ cleanses us from all sin—Jn. 19:34; 1 Pet. 1:18–20

Ministers only administer what is visible—Matt. 3:11; 1 Cor. 3:5, 7; Rom. 6:3–4

The Lord gives the cleansing that is signified in the sacrament—Eph. 5:26; Acts 22:16; 1 Pet. 3:21; Gal. 3:27; 1 Cor. 12:13; Eph. 4:22–24

Baptism in the name of the Trinity should not be repeated as the

Anabaptists require—Mark 16:16; Matt. 28:19; Eph. 4:5; Heb. 6:2; Acts 2:38; 8:16

Baptism not in the name of the Trinity needs to be performed if it was not done before—Acts 19:3–5

Infants should receive baptism just as the children of Israel were circumcised as infants—Gen. 17:11–12; Matt. 19:14; 1 Cor. 7:14; Acts 2:39; 16:15, 33

Jesus shed His blood no less for the children of believers than for adult persons—Acts 2:39; Col. 2:11–12

In the law a lamb was to be sacrificed for children shortly after birth to show that they were partakers of the sacrament of Christ's suffering and death—Lev. 12:6; Jn. 1:29

Baptism is called the "circumcision" of Christ—Col. 2:11

35. THE HOLY SUPPER

Instituted by our Lord Jesus Christ—Matt. 26:26; Mk. 14:22; Lk. 22:19; 1 Cor. 11:23–25

To be administered to those who are regenerated—Jn. 3:5–6; and believe the Gospel—Jn. 5:23, 25; 1 Cor. 11:27–30

This life is peculiar to God's elect—1 Jn. 5:12; Jn. 10:28

As we are nourished by faith in Christ, the Holy Supper symbolizes the nourishment of His broken body and shed blood—Jn. 6:35, 53–58, 63–64; 1 Cor. 10:16–17; Eph. 3:17

We do not partake of Christ physically, but by the Spirit through faith we eat the flesh of Christ and drink His blood—Jn. 6:55–56; 1 Cor. 10:16; Acts 3:21; Mk. 16:19; Matt. 26:11

We partake of the merits of His suffering and death—1 Cor. 10:2–4; 11:26; Isa. 55:2; Rom. 8:22–23

The unregenerate are not to take this supper lest they eat and drink judgment to themselves—1 Cor. 11:27–29; 2:14; 2 Cor. 6:14–15

36. CIVIL GOVERNMENT

Government on all levels is appointed by God—Ex. 18:20ff.; Rom. 13:1; Prov. 8:15; Jer. 21:12; 22:2–3; Ps. 82:1, 6; 101:2ff.; Deut. 1:15–16; 16:18; 17:15; Dan. 2:21, 37; 5:18

The duty of government is to watch for the welfare of the state and protect the sacred ministry—Isa. 49:25; 1 Kg. 15:12; 2 Kg. 23:2–4; Rom. 13:14

Everyone must be subject to the government Titus 3:1; Rom. 13:1, 5

Pay tribute—Mk. 12:17; Matt. 17:24–27; Rom. 13:6–7

Obey all laws not contrary to the Word of God—Acts 4:17–19; 5:29; Hos. 5:11; Dan. 3:16–18

Pray for rulers—Jer. 29:7; 1 Tim. 2:1, 2 Titus 3:1; Heb. 13:17–18

Have respect for the dignity of government—2 Pet. 2:10; Jude 8, 10

37. THE LAST JUDGMENT

Christ will return as He ascended visibly and bodily into heaven—Acts 1:11

At a time appointed by the Lord, unknown to us—Matt. 24:36; 25:13; 1 Thess. 5:1–2; Rev. 6:11; Acts 1:7; 2 Pet. 3:10

He will come in glory and in judgment—2 Thess. 1:7–8; Acts 17:31; Matt. 24:30; 25:31; Jude 15; 2 Pet. 4:5; 2 Tim. 4:1; 2 Pet. 3:7, 10

All men and women and children will appear before Him—Rev. 20:12–13; Acts 17:31; Heb. 6:2; 9:27; 2 Cor. 5:10; Rom. 14:10

The voice of the archangel and the sound of the trumpet will summon all men—1 Cor. 15:43; 1 Thess. 4:16; Rev. 20:12–13

The souls of the dead will reunite with their bodies—Jn. 5:28–29; 6:54; Dan. 12:2; Job 19:26–27—and the living will be changed instantly into incorruption—1 Cor. 15:51–53

All men will be judged by what they have done in this life—whether it be good or bad—Rev. 20:12–13; 1 Cor. 4:5; Rom. 14:11–12; Job 34:11; Jn. 5:24, 29; Dan. 12:2; Ps. 62:13; Matt. 11:22; 23:33; Rom. 2:1–2, 5–6, 16; 2 Cor. 5:10; Heb. 6:2; 9:27; Jude 15; Matt. 7:1–2; 12:36

This judgment will be terrible for the ungodly—Rev. 6:15–16; Heb. 10:27; Matt. 13:41–42, 49–50; 25:41; Lk. 13:28; 1 Cor. 6:9–10

This judgment will be desirable and comfortable for the elect—Lk. 14:14; 21:28; 1 Jn. 3:2; 4:17; 2 Thess. 1:5, 7; Rev. 21:3–4

They shall see God's holy vengeance upon their enemies who persecuted them—Matt. 25:46; 2 Thess. 1:6–8; Mal. 4:3; Lk. 16:22–26; Rev. 21:8; 2 Pet. 2:9

They will be crowned with glory and honor—Matt. 25:34; 13:43

Christ will confess their names before His Father—Matt. 10:32

All tears will be wiped away from their eyes—Rev. 21:4; Isa. 25:8

They will enjoy a glory that they have never imagined—Isa. 64:4; 1 Cor. 2:9

The return of Christ is the believer's most ardent desire and the fulfillment of all the promises of God—Heb. 10:36–38; Rev. 22:20

Summary of
The Canons of Dort

෨

*This summary is written to facilitate a quick reference for the study
of the various doctrines contained in the Canons of Dort.*

FIRST HEAD OF DOCTRINE
Divine Election and Reprobation
("Unconditional Election")

1. God would be just to leave all men in their sin and condemn all men.

2. God shows His sovereign love in the sending of Jesus Christ.

3. In mercy, God sends ministers to preach the Gospel to all men.

4. Unbelievers perish in their sins while believers of the Gospel are saved.

5. God is not guilty for man's sin; God is the Author, not of sin, but of faith and salvation.

6. God eternally decreed before the foundation of the world who is elected (chosen) for salvation and who shall perish in their sin.

7. Election is defined as a gracious, sovereign act of God by which He chooses a certain number of persons to redemption in Christ.

8. God's election is one—both in the Old and New Testaments.

9. Election is not founded on any good conditions which man may later demonstrate and which God is able to foresee.

10. Election is by the good pleasure of God's perfect will.

11. God's election is unalterable.

12. The fruits of faith eventually give assurance of one's election.

13. Assurance of election does not make believers careless or callous, but humble and faithful in their service of love and thanksgiving.

14. The doctrine of election was preached in both the Old and New Testaments and should be taught in the Church of God today.

15. Those not elected by God are passed by in God's eternal decree (the decree of Reprobation), and are left to continue in their sin unto condemnation.

16. Those who continue in using the means of grace, yet do not have an assured confidence of soul should not be alarmed nor doubt their election nor fear that they might be reprobate. Those who persevere in the faith prove their election, while those who cast off the faith prove their reprobation.

17. Believers ought not to doubt the election and salvation of their children, who are members of the Covenant of Grace.

18. The Scriptures teach us that it is dishonoring to God to doubt that He has the right to show grace to the elect and condemn the reprobate.

REJECTION OF ERRORS
WITH REGARD TO THE DOCTRINE OF ELECTION

The Synod rejects...

1. the error of having election based upon foreseen faith and perseverance in faith by man.

2. the error of saying that there are two kinds of election—one more general which brings men to faith (who later could be lost), and another more definite election which results in salvation.

3. the error that faith is a condition to salvation.

4. the error which says that election depends on how men use the light of nature, or makes it dependent on pious living.

5. the error which says that complete and decisive election depends upon foreseen perseverance in faith (ie. man's perseverance is a condition for God's election).

6. the error that those elected may still perish.

7. the error that the elect may never be certain of their election.

8. the error that God did not pass by any men and thus leave them in their state of condemnation.

9. the error that certain nations are better than others and therefore God shows grace to them and excludes others.

THE SECOND HEAD OF DOCTRINE
THE DEATH OF CHRIST, AND THE REDEMPTION OF MAN THEREBY
("LIMITED ATONEMENT")

1. God's justice requires that all sin, since it is against His high majesty, must be punished with everlasting punishment of body and soul.

2. Since we could not satisfy God's perfect justice by ourselves, He sent His Son to make full satisfaction in man's place.

3. Christ's death is the only satisfaction for sin—sufficient to cleanse the whole world of sin, but efficient for the elect.

4. Christ's death was perfect because He was truly God and man.

5. The Gospel of Christ must be preached to all men.

6. Those who reject the Gospel do so because of their sin and not because the work of Christ was insufficient.

7. Believers have faith solely by the grace of God given to them from eternity—not by their own merit.

8. God's purpose in Jesus Christ is to make the death of Christ efficient

(effectual) in the saving of His elect only.

9. This purpose of God continues to be accomplished, regardless of all opposition, for the gathering of the Church which will always exist with Christ as the foundation. This Church will praise God both in time and eternity.

REJECTION OF ERRORS
WITH REGARD TO LIMITED ATONEMENT

The Synod rejects...

1. the error of those who say that Christ did not die to save anyone in particular, and hold to the possibility that Christ's death would be perfect even if no one believed.

2. the error of those who deny that God confirmed the New Covenant of grace through the blood of Jesus.

3. the error of those who say that Christ's satisfaction did not merit salvation itself, but only allowed the Father to make new conditions which depend upon man's free will.

4. the error that says that Christ's death allowed God to remove the demand for a perfect obedience in faith, but allows imperfect faith to be considered as a perfect obedience to the law.

5. the error of those who say that no one is worthy of condemnation due to original sin, because all men are in the Covenant of Grace.

6. the error that man's free will may combine with God's grace to bring about salvation.

7. the error that says Christ did not die for the elect, since they do not need the death of Christ.

THE THIRD AND FOURTH HEADS OF DOCTRINE
THE CORRUPTION OF MAN, HIS CONVERSION TO GOD,
AND THE MANNER THEREOF
("TOTAL DEPRAVITY" AND "IRRESISTIBLE GRACE")

1. Man was created perfectly in the image of God, but the fall into sin totally involved him in all that is contrary to perfection.

2. All of Adam's posterity are corrupt by nature, Christ excepted.

3. All men are conceived and born in sin and without the Holy Spirit are neither willing nor able to return to God.

4. Man still has a knowledge of God in natural things, but it cannot bring him to a saving knowledge of God and he cannot use it properly even in things natural and civil. In the end, this "light" proclaims man guilty and leaves him inexcusable before God.

5. The law reveals man's sin, but cannot save him.

6. Nature and the law do not save, but God saves in the Old and New Testaments by the operation of the Holy Spirit through the preaching of the Gospel.

7. By the sovereign good pleasure of God, salvation is revealed to many who are to respond with humble and grateful hearts.

8. The Gospel is to be preached to all men sincerely.

9. Because of sin within man, they reject the Gospel or allow other cares and pleasures to choke it out. This is not the fault of the Gospel.

10. Those who believe the Gospel do so, not by their fallen free wills, but by the effectual call of God.

11. The Holy Spirit effectually regenerates the heart, gives new qualities to the will, brings the dead heart to life, and gives the gift of faith to God's elect.

12. Repentance and faith is a supernatural work of God the Holy Spirit in man whereby the will of man is activated and able to repent and believe.

13. This working of God in man is a wondrous mystery, yet man believes it by the grace of God.

14. Faith is the gift of God—infused, inbreathed into man. God produces both the will to believe and the act of believing.

15. God owes salvation to nobody. The believer, therefore, owes eternal gratitude to God and must pray to God for others who remain in unbelief.

16. Regeneration by the Holy Spirit does not take away the will of man so that he becomes just a "senseless stock and block", but it renews the will of man, enabling him to make a responsible confession of faith.

17. The gift of faith from God does not exclude, but includes the continued use of the means of grace—the admonitions of the Gospel, the influence (preaching and study) of the Word, the sacraments, and church discipline. God uses these means to bring us to faith, and we must continue in them.

REJECTION OF ERRORS
WITH REGARD TO TOTAL DEPRAVITY AND IRRESISTIBLE GRACE

The Synod rejects...

1. the error that teaches that original sin does not condemn all men.

2. the error that says that man did not possess goodness, righteousness, and holiness as a part of his will before the Fall, and that, therefore, these were not lost from the will of man after the Fall.

3. the error of those who say that the will of man was not affected by the Fall.

4. the error that says that man is not totally dead in sin, but can still turn to God under his own power.

5. the error that man can gradually move from the common grace of God to the saving grace of God by himself.

6. the error of those who say that man's will after conversion is essentially no different, and therefore, faith is not a gift of God but an act of man (except in the power given by God to attain it).

7. the error of those who say that the grace of God in our conversion is only advisory—directing us, rather than performing a real work within us.

8. the error of those who say that man may resist God and the Holy Spirit in the matter of regeneration.

9. the error that says that grace and free will of man initiate conversion, and that God does not begin to work in man until man in his free will moves first.

THE FIFTH HEAD OF DOCTRINE
"THE PERSEVERANCE OF THE SAINTS"

1. Those whom God has called into Christ, and regenerated, he also delivers from the dominion of sin, while in this life there remain the infirmities of the flesh.

2. The weakness of the flesh and daily sin causes even the best works of the saints to be blemished with sin in order to humble men and drive them to Christ for refuge. The result must be mortification of the flesh, piety, and a striving for the goal of perfection which will be reached after this life.

3. Believers, because of this indwelling sin, could not remain faithful if left to themselves. It is God who is faithful to mercifully confirm and powerfully to preserve the saints, even to the end.

4. Man in the weakness of his flesh must be watchful and prayerful that he will not reject the influence that God exerts in his life, and thereby fall into great sin. Although the saints backslide, they are not ultimately lost (cf. David and Peter).

5. When the saints fall into grave sin, their faith is weakened and they lose their sense of God's favor until they repent and turn to God again.

6. God does not change His purpose of election and allow sinners to utterly fall away by withdrawing His Holy Spirit, thus allowing them to fall into everlasting destruction.

7. God does not remove the seed of regeneration (the Holy Spirit), and by His Word and Holy Spirit works repentance in the hearts of those He has elected that they might return humbly unto Him in faith.

8. It is not by the merits or strength of man, but by the free mercy of God that man does not totally fall away from God and perish. Man, left to himself would surely perish eternally, but God never deserts His chosen ones nor revokes His eternal purpose.

9. Believers do obtain the assurance of faith which says that they will forever be members of the Church, have forgiveness of sins, and everlasting life.

10. Assurance of salvation comes from faith in the promises of the Gospel, which are worked in us by the Word and the Spirit of God, and from a

holy desire to preserve a good conscience and perform good works.

11. Believers struggle with various carnal doubts and do not always feel the full force of this assurance, but God will never tempt them above their ability to bear it, but makes for them a way of escape; also the Holy Spirit works assurance in us.

12. This doctrine of perseverance (that the saints may never be lost) does not work pride in man, but works humility, reverence, piety, patience, prayer, endurance in suffering, confession of the truth, and rejoicing.

13. Those who are recovered from backsliding are not filled with pride, but take greater care lest they be allowed to fall into more grievous torment and God turn His face from them again.

14. What work God has begun by the preaching of the Gospel, He will perfect by the hearing and reading of the Word, by meditations, teachings, warnings, by promises of the Word, and by the holy sacraments.

15. The carnal (unconverted) mind is not able to comprehend this doctrine, and thus mock and ridicule it, but the saints of God take great comfort in it.

REJECTION OF ERRORS
WITH REGARD TO THE PERSEVERANCE OF THE SAINTS

The Synod rejects...

1. the error that says perseverance is not the fruit of election, but a condition of the New Covenant which man must fulfill by his own free will.

2. the error of those who say that God gives man the power to persevere, but that man has the free will to accept or deny this power of God.

3. the error that teaches that man can and often does fall from justifying faith and from grace and salvation.

4. the error that says that true believers can commit the unforgivable sin against the Holy Spirit and hence be lost eternally.

5 the error that says that without further revelation of God we have no certainty of our perseverance in faith.

6. the error that says that this doctrine of perseverance causes men to live lives of low morals and prayerlessness.

7. the error that says that a temporary faith (not a true, saving faith) is the same as true faith for as long as it exists.

8. the error that says that a person could be regenerated more than once.

9. the error that claims that Christ nowhere prayed that believers should continue in faith.

CONCLUDING STATEMENT

*"The doctrine of this creed is drawn from the Word of God and is in harmony
with other Reformed creeds of the day. The Synod rejects the notion that the
doctrine of God's sovereign grace set forth in the creed gives cause for men to
sin or have a false sense of assurance. Likewise it does not make God either
arbitrary or the author of sin. To the enemies of the Reformed churches, a
warning is issued not to misrepresent these teachings. Adherents to the creed
are likewise exhorted to further these teachings, and warned to take care that
these doctrines are taught within the limits herein set forth, that the piety and
holiness of Christian lives may bring glory to God."*

*"May Jesus Christ, the son of God, who, seated at the Father's right hand, gives
gifts to men, sanctify us in the truth: bring to the truth those who err; shut the
mouths of the calumniators of sound doctrine, and endue the faithful ministers
of his Word with the spirit of wisdom and discretion, that all their discourses
may tend to the glory of God, and the edification of those who hear them.
Amen."*

Made in the USA
Las Vegas, NV
03 December 2020

11949749R10079